George W Perrie, C. G Rosenberg

Buckskin Mose

Life from the Lakes to the Pacific

George W Perrie, C. G Rosenberg

Buckskin Mose

Life from the Lakes to the Pacific

ISBN/EAN: 9783743686762

Printed in Europe, USA, Canada, Australia, Japan

Cover: Foto ©ninafisch / pixelio.de

More available books at **www.hansebooks.com**

BUCKSKIN MOSE;

OR,

LIFE FROM THE LAKES TO THE PACIFIC,

AS

ACTOR, CIRCUS-RIDER, DETECTIVE, RANGER, GOLD-DIGGER, INDIAN SCOUT, AND GUIDE.

WRITTEN BY HIMSELF.

"There are more things in heaven and earth, Horatio,
Than are dreamt of in your philosophy."—HAMLET.

EDITED, AND WITH ILLUSTRATIONS,
BY C. G. ROSENBERG.

NEW YORK:
HENRY L. HINTON, PUBLISHER, 744 BROADWAY.
1873.

Stereotyped at the
WOMEN'S PRINTING HOUSE,
56, 58 and 60 Park Street,
New York.

PREFACE.

As a young author, although scarcely what the world would consider a young man, I should scarcely feel inclined to say a word in presenting this volume to it, were it not that I wish the public to comprehend one of the two reasons which have induced me to write it. As it would be idle, even for a man of decided literary genius, to deny that pecuniary profit is, in most instances, the incentive to the exercise of his power, so, in a humbler fashion (for I consider myself a man of no genius), I will scarcely affirm that I do not look with a degree of longing on the possible success of my first effort.

Let me, however, frankly say that I have another and a stronger reason for writing this work.

While hoping that I have not thrust this into undue prominence, as I have, in every case, made it secondary to the facts which are detailed, it is my wish to demonstrate to the public of the United States, that the manner in which the Government protects the settler is neither good for him nor for the Indian. It must equally fail in satisfying its children and its vassals. At times, it leaves the first totally unprotected. When they grow accustomed to the habit of self-protection, it not infrequently represses the sturdy independence thus begotten, instead of guiding it by the ability, wisdom, and honesty of its appointed officials. In like manner, it has no settled course of policy with the latter. At one time it bribes, and at another, it lashes them into subjection.

Perhaps, the settler is not entirely elevated in character, nor the Indian thoroughly debased. But this wavering and uncertain line of policy cannot do otherwise than lower the nature of the first, while it certainly cannot raise that of the last.

That one considers his Government as weak and capricious, while this one believes it to be both tyrannical and asinine.

In addition to this, those who are selected to command the troops employed in the neighborhood of the Reservations, or to act as Indian Agents, are, in nine cases out of ten, utterly ignorant of the nature of the savage with whom they have to deal, the character of the country in which they have to move; and, in the latter position, not infrequently deficient in one of the cardinal virtues—that of honesty. In this last case, they will not only disgust the settler, but enrage the savage, who, on the score of his own dishonesty and treachery, is far less disposed to smile at these vices in others, when he himself suffers from their exercise. The false philanthropy, also, is deeply injurious, which believes in the possibility of guiding uneducated nature without a due degree of compulsory restriction.

If in mentioning these few points in relation to the dealings of our Government with the white settler and the red-skin, I awaken the attention of the public to the real obstacles for the preservation of a steady and creditable peace on the Indian territory and in the Reservations, without the complete extermination of the original inhabitants of my country, I shall be satisfied. Nor do I feel that I have said nearly as much, nor said it one-tenth as strongly, as the necessity for plain speaking might have justified me in doing.

Before concluding, I would, however, call attention to one portion of my volume which, without corroborative proof, might cause considerable doubt as to my veracity. This is my positive mention of the existence of Masonry, of my own knowledge, among the Cheyennes, and by hearsay from them, among other Western tribes.

If I am right, it was in 1854, that Judge Harrison, of Red Bluffs, in California, with his wife and children, was captured by the Cheyennes. Like myself, he was a Mason, and was indebted to that circumstance for the liberation of himself and his family. This he told me in Susanville, where he afterwards died. When he mentioned this circumstance to me, he showed me a war-club presented to him, which was almost identical in its decorative carving with my own, and which is now, or lately was, in the possession of his widow. Nor have I any reason to doubt that there may be others now living, who have also been indebted, for a similar immunity, to the fact of their belonging to the Masonic order.

While touching upon this, I might also mention that Peter Lassen, killed by the Indians, at Black Rock, in 1859, was the first Mason who carried a Charter to, and founded the first Masonic Lodge, on the Pacific coast. Peace be with the old man's ashes.

ILLUSTRATIONS.

	PAGE
How I sold Pop-corn	16
My Capture of Jackson	31
Spotting a Counterfeiter	34
A second Offer of Marriage	63
My first Appearance in Susanville	92
A Struggle for Life	125
The Monument erected to Peter Lassen in Honey Lake Valley	102
Being requested to change Trees	119
Bound to the Stake	140
An unexpected Ally	155
Clo-ke-ta's Warning	222
Taking Payment	249

CHAPTER I.

My First Experience in the Circus—An Accident and a Change of Calling—Family Affection—Pop-corn—A Little Cheek, and a Great Deal of Dismay—Success as a Dealer in Grain—Being an Actor—Caught Again—Blood, and its Consequences—Bailed Out, and In Again—The Good-natured Irishman—Change of Venue—Another Profession.

Actor, trapper, scout, gold-digger, and guide, my life, very unlike that of most of my readers, has been one of plenty of change and adventure, but certainly not of money-making. They say "A rolling stone gathers no moss." I have had good reason to feel this proverbial truth, having been a wanderer on the face, if not of this earth, at all events, of this continent.

My earliest recollection, which is worth my own remembrance, is a decidedly unpleasant one. When no more than eight years of age I was connected with the Circus of Dan Rice. Necessarily, I was a very unimportant member of it; and not feeling that it was in every respect what I thought a circus-life ought to be, I took it into my head to run away from it. Before I had covered sufficient ground to get out of the agent's reach, he caught me, and I had the gratification of being very well and soundly flogged. The smart of this judicial visitation upon my skin still recurs to me at times, and renders the locality in Kentucky, where the flogging took place, a very sore spot in my memory. I consequently will not name it.

In spite of this escapade, I gradually became a proficient in bare-back riding, vaulting, on the slack-rope and in the trapeze-performance, excelling all the boys attached to the circus, and in consequence became the pet of Old Dan, with whom I remained for three years. My youthful ambition to shine in this career was, however, brought to an untimely close. An uncle of mine discovered me on the Mississippi, and immediately wrote to my father, who, at the time I left home, had been the landlord of the United States Hotel in Galena. Making a somewhat wrathful pilgrimage in search of his missing offspring, he caught up with me at some small place in Kentucky, reclaimed me from the vocation of my choice, and after taking me home and chastising me in a truly parental fashion, bound me out as an apprentice to the village blacksmith. It would be needless to say, that the forge was by no means as pleasant an occupation, to my youthful mind, as the daring life on the sawdust of the arena.

Some six months after, I forgot the parental scourge, and wrote a letter to the manager of Older and Orton's Circus, which was then performing at Portage City, Wisconsin.

What sort of a letter it was, I can now scarcely tell. But my education had not been remarkable in its extent, and it may be presumed the orthography as well as the calligraphy, possibly, astonished him who received it. If so, he never mentioned the fact to me, but returned me a favorable answer. Consequently, I once more made tracks, and joined them for the season.

Here I was so successful, and became such a general favorite, that I received the offer of a star-engagement from Levi North, with whom I remained until an injury received on the occasion of my benefit, in the execution of an unusually daring feat of horsemanship, brought our connection to an end. The company were obliged to leave me behind them in Chicago.

My recovery was slow and tedious. Although my professional brethren displayed great kindness to me, in every way, the means I had made, even with their assistance, were insufficient for my needs. Once or twice, I thought of writing to my relatives in Galena.

The supposable wrath of my paternal proprietor, however, deterred me from doing so. The shiver of filial fear at his retributive justice induced me to make an effort to support myself in a new field. This was in a grocery store at the corner of Randolph and Deerborne streets, kept by a man named Martin. It was a widely different sphere of exertion from that in which my previous employment had been cast, as well as one even more different from that in which I was afterwards to make my mark. Often, since, I have laughed over this period of my life. In the Forge and the Circus, I had learnt much which might fit me for my future. But, it is somewhat curious for Buckskin Mose ever to have figured in peddling or carrying out tea and sugar, potted fruits and whiskey, with other such necessaries and luxuries, from a corner-grocery.

But I was not destined to continue at this work for any length of time. One day, a fire occurred on the premises, and in endeavoring to rescue a keg of brandy from the flames, I slipped upon the ice in front of the store—it was then midwinter—and broke my arm.

This untoward accident threw me again out of employment, and I remember my angry feelings while the doctor was placing my maimed limb in splints, and I was thinking what I could do for a living. Some few days after, when, worn out by the suffering and compulsory inaction consequent upon this accident, I was wandering through the streets, I stumbled upon another uncle of mine.

He was one of the millionnaires of Chicago. As many men have grown rich by the sudden growth of the cities in which they live, rather than by their own efforts, he had gained his dollars. But in doing so, he had forgotten his love for those who bore his name. At any rate, he had done so for me, as far as extending me any helping hand in my immediate necessity.

"You must work, my boy! Only see what I have done. No friends assisted me. I began at the lowest rung of the ladder, and now I am pretty well off in the world. God bless you!"

Then he tapped me on the shoulder in a benevolent manner, and walked on, never thinking of assisting the beneficence he had asked to bless me.

But I had to live. With my broken arm, what was there left for me to attempt? Davy Crockett mentions the shell-corn business at one period of his eventful life, as having suggested itself to him. Why should not I become a pop-corn merchant in a humble approach to the calling the hero of Kentucky had once followed. But, to my intense disgust, on diligent inquiry, I could find no pop-corn in the whole of Chicago, whether for love or money, save in one store. The amount demanded for this was thirty dollars. Of the last article mentioned above—money—I had none. Of the first, I had plenty. But this was not a circulating medium. As, with my unlamed hand, I was scraping my forehead in the hope of exhuming an idea, I looked up and found myself in front of a grocery store. Its owner was standing behind the counter. His face wore a benevolent and kindly expression. At no time in my life, from that in which I ran away from Dan Rice's Circus, have I been long in forming a determination. So I walked in, and asked him for the loan of the money, with which I intended to monopolize the pop-corn trade.

"Thirty dollars!" he exclaimed.

He was profoundly astonished, and on reflection, I am compelled to say, well he might be.

"That's the exact sum I want," was my answer.

"But, young fellow! you're an entire stranger to me."

"So you are to me," I undauntedly replied. "I don't know you from Adam or any other fellow. But I like your face, and so, if you want a lift, I don't mind taking you with me into the pop-corn business."

He smiled. His smile was indeed a full-fed and jolly laugh.

"Well!" he said, "upon my word, I rather like your frank cheek. We'll go and see about it."

The result of the inquiries of Mr. Dobbs, the grocer in question, was that he not only advanced me the money to purchase the whole stock, but allowed me to store the corn in his own establishment. At the time it did not strike me as being so, but was doubtless the result of a sagacious forethought, as, should I fail in keeping my daily accounts square, he could easily foreclose on my stock-in-trade. Be this as it may, Mr. Dobbs did more for me. All well-regulated communities indulge in the licensing business—to a greater or less extent. So did, and probably does, Chicago. The unlicensed sale of pop-corn would have been a risky affair. When he told me this, my face fell. How was I to get a license.

Mr. Dobbs was equal to the emergency on this occasion, also.

"Come along with me to the Mayor."

It was the first occasion on which I had ever stood in the actual presence of such a high civic dignitary. The introduction was an era in my life. It would have been in that of any boy. The reader may therefore imagine that my equanimity, which my new friend had thought proper to denominate "cheek," felt somewhat abashed, as the magistrate looked up from his desk, and gazing, as I fancied, sternly at me, said:

"What is the matter now, Mr. Dobbs?"

"Mr. Mayor," responded Mr. Dobbs, "I wish to introduce to you a young friend of mine, who wishes to take out a license to sell pop-corn."

"It will be a hundred and fifty dollars."

I looked from the Mayor to my new friend. One hundred and fifty dollars! Where was the money to come from? I never before felt so near whimpering. Very certainly, I have never since. My boyhood must be remembered, as an apology for this tendency on my part. I was unable, in the extremity of my trouble, to utter a word of entreaty.

"He has no money, Mr. Mayor!" answered Mr. Dobbs. "So you must deal as kindly as possible with him."

The magistrate laughed, not at what my friend had said, but at my painful look of dismay. Mr. Dobbs also chuckled slightly. Then the Mayor observed:

"I will see what can be done for the lad. He seems a bright young fellow."

After saying this, he named the most liberal terms for the license, and when it was made out by his clerk and Mr. Dobbs had paid for it, with a very low bow, I turned to leave the office. At this moment a gentleman entered, whom the Mayor introduced to my benefactor. After doing so, he was beginning to mention what I had come to him for, when the new-comer turned to me, saying:

"Why, I know this young lad. He is my nephew."

The Mayor gazed at me and Mr. Dobbs, with some considerable surprise, as he ejaculated:

"Indeed!"

I felt that my face had crimsoned up to the very roots of my hair, but my reply was prompt and very bitter:

"You are entirely wrong, sir!"

It was impossible for me to avoid recalling the fact that he had not made me the slightest offer of assistance, while my generous benefactor had not only loaned me money, but given me some three hours of his time—the last, possibly, being the greatest amount of kindness.

"How?" said my uncle, knitting his brows. "Are not you the son of Mr. ——, of Galena?"

"Yes."

"And you were born there?"

"Of course, I was."

"Your father had a brother in this city?"

"I know he had."

"Then, I am that brother and your uncle. You know it, for you spoke to me only yesterday."

"Did I?" was my angry exclamation.

Making another bow to the Mayor, I turned and

walked out, leaving my disgusted uncle to stare, and, if he was given to profanity, to swear after me.

The pop-corn business, so strangely commenced, grew and prospered. From my one small basket, it gradually extended itself. At last a regiment—or rather one small company of boys—with cans containing it, with the name of "Mose" painted on them, strapped upon their shoulders, sold pop-corn in the streets, the cars, the theatres, and the hotels. Why or how I came to take the name of "Mose," it is perhaps difficult to say. But I had commenced life in the Circus, when the "Mose" of Chanfrau was an universally quoted name throughout the country. It had been my name on the bills with Dan Rice, Older and Orton, and Levi North. Remaining in my memory, it probably stuck to me when I embarked in my new calling.

Comparative wealth seemed to be pouring in on me. In a measure, I was becoming not only a lad of means, but somewhat locally celebrated under the name of my adoption.

To account for my rapidly gaining money, it must be remembered that one bushel of shelled, makes eleven of popped corn. My profits were consequently in proportion, even if the whole trade of Chicago, in this thriftily manufactured commodity, had not been in my hands.

With the termination of my winter's sale of pop-corn which closed, I may state, with gratification, with as much gain for the good Mr. Dobbs as for myself, I had again to think of employment. Luckily, the results of my two accidents were now entirely healed, and although I could scarcely have risked appearing yet in the circus, I saw no reason to preclude me from going behind the

"The pop-corn business, so strangely commenced, grew and prospered.—*Page* 16.

footlights. After some difficulty, theatricals being less overstocked then, than now, I obtained an engagement at Rice's, latterly known as MacVicker's Theatre.

It was here decided that comic business was my "line," and the public, not unnaturally, were more than kind to one whom pop-corn had made a sort of favorite.

However, it was not until the following winter that a positive success rewarded me in my new profession. I had been offered an engagement by Langrish and Atwater, of Wisconsin, and accepted it. This was when I had nearly reached the rawly ripe age of sixteen. These managers gave me every chance of displaying what talent I chanced to have. Not only were such parts as *Ragged Pat* and the *Irish Tutor* intrusted to me, but I shone also with, I now suspect, a somewhat doubtful light in "The Flying Dutchman," "The Spectre Bridegroom," "Nick of the Woods," and "Ten Nights in a Bar-room." Irishman, Dutchman, Cockney, Yorkshireman, and Yankee all came indifferently to my share.

Bright visions of future reputation as a legitimate actor began to rise upon me; but at the close of this season, the difficulty of procuring another engagement forced me to become a theatrical Arab in Yankee Simpson's travelling company.

After a brief wandering under their tent, I dissolved my connection with it, and returned to my last year's Eldorado—Chicago. The reason for my taking this step, it is unnecessary to put in print. The theatrical profession will readily divine it, when they are told that shortly after, I formed a not unimportant member of a joint-stock travelling company, which for the next six months ran through Illinois and Wisconsin. We had reached Racine, in the latter State, when our co-operative speculation came to a sudden end. One morning, on quitting our virtuous couches, we found that the bed on which our treasurer reposed had not been tenanted. The vagabond had "absquatulated" with the whole of the joint-stock funds.

Here was a situation for the future Forrests, Placides, Broughams, and Jeffersons of the American stage—for, as such, we considered ourselves. We were "dead broke."

Four of these budding reputations, Wolf, Sam Ryan, McManus, and myself, were tendered by the tender-hearted public a Benefit, to rescue us from our financial difficulties. It need scarcely be said with what a buoyant sense of gratitude its pecuniary results were received by us.

Once more, I struck for Chicago. It was in a bee-line.

It need scarcely be explained that I, at any rate, was heartily sick of the joint-stock travelling business in theatricals.

Here, old Dan Emmett, of Emmett's Varieties, in Randolph Street, Chicago, gave me a short engagement, after the close of which I accompanied Maggie Mitchell to Milwaukie, where I played with that lady at the Academy of Music.

The engagement had been for Miss Mitchell most successful, when one evening my horror may be imagined at seeing the face of my father among the audience in front of the scenes. For the moment, I felt as if I should be glad to see the stage open, and sink through it. My tongue seemed cleaving to the roof of my mouth. How I got through my part, it would be impossible to say. But I managed to do so, and was in my dressing-room when the call-boy entered and informed me a gentleman was waiting to see me.

"Why was he let in?" I roared out.

"Please; Mister! he said he wanted to see you on most important business."

Rushing to the window of the dressing-room, I looked out. It was no use of thinking of escape, that way. The room was on the third story. A leap from it was not to be thought of, even if the loose brick and timber piled at the base of the wall of the theatre had not rendered it doubly a mad experiment. Delaying as long as I could, I was at last forced to descend. It was, on my part, a decidedly unrehearsed scene in real life.

I do not like to speak of my father's remonstrance, or the tears which accompanied his appeal to me to return home. My pride prevented me from weeping, but it could scarcely do so. And, indeed, when he took some considerable blame to himself for having thrown me upon this (as he was pleased to call it) vagabond life, I am not quite certain that my eyes were not wet as well as his.

Suffice it, that, at the close of my present engagement, I consented to comply with his wishes, and renounce the stage. Then, and only then, he left me.

On my way home, at the close of the performances, in Milwaukie, of Maggie Mitchell, I had determined to pause for a day or two with a friend who was then in Waukegan. Lewis was considerably older than myself, and since we had first met I had become much attached to him, as youth generally does to greater years when they choose to associate with it. Here occurred my third physical misadventure.

One evening, while walking, with him, down the principal street, a man, in company with several others, accosted him.

What words were interchanged between them, I can scarcely recollect. All I know, is, that it was one of those inexplicable quarrels which arise about females.

They came to blows, and endeavoring to separate the two, I received a heavy one upon my jaw from a slung-shot, which knocked out two of my back teeth, and stretched me senseless on the ground. After this I knew nothing more, save that when I recovered consciousness I was led to the room of Lewis, by himself. While lying upon the bed, not yet aware of the full extent of the injury done me, I was recalled to my complete senses by a terrific clamor in the street. Then, for the first time, I learnt from Lewis that he had made short work of one of the gang who had attacked him, by stabbing him fatally.

The infuriated populace had followed us, and had determined upon lynching both, as speedily as possible.

Lewis looked white, and fearfully scared, as he listened to their savage yells. But it must frankly be owned that I was as thoroughly scared as he was; although I retained my presence of mind, leapt from the bed, and was about barricading the door of the apartment—because it would have been impossible to prevent them entering the house. Then there came a momentary pause, and the voice of some one having authority was heard in the street, addressing the crowd.

"Thank Heaven!" cried Lewis. "It is the sheriff."

The pause, however, had only been momentary. So wild was the fierce burst of derision that followed, I almost thought my companion had been premature in his thankfulness. There was a fierce struggle audible without, which lasted for some few minutes, and then the sheriff and his officers were victorious. They demanded admittance in the name of the law, and after entering the house, arrested Lewis on the charge of murder, and myself as an accomplice.

A brief examination, however, soon proved my complete innocence, and I was discharged, but ordered to give bonds for my appearance against my friend. Of course I was unable to provide the requisite sureties, being an entire stranger; and in consequence was locked up in the debtors' prison. Here was a situation. With my face swollen from the effects of the blow, two of my teeth knocked out, and my lip and nose fearfully cut, and incarcerated because I could not get bail! Lewis, nevertheless, did not desert me. A stranger in Waukegan who had seen me in Milwaukee, and had heard part of my story from a friend of my father's, recognized my name, and after verifying my identity by ocular proof (it must have been somewhat difficult in my then disfigured condition), wrote the particulars of my trouble to him. He had but just returned to Galena, and was daily expecting me. Only judge what my surprise must have been, on seeing him one fine morning appear in the place of my confinement. If on our last encounter I would have avoided him, what would I not now have given to have escaped seeing him; under such circumstances.

It seemed, however, that my fears of his reproaches were wrong. He gave bail for my appearance upon the trial at the next term, and took me home with him, without uttering a single reproach.

Perhaps, as I have since imagined, he may have

thought all such reproach would have been useless with such a confirmed "ne'er-do-weel" as he must perforce have believed me.

At the time appointed I, of course, reappeared in Waukegan. Unfortunately my father had been unable to leave his home, never for an instant imagining his services might again be required. Owing, however, to the incompetency of the District Attorney or the astuteness of my friend's counsel, the trial of the latter was deferred until the succeeding term of Court; and what was my disgust at finding, having surrendered on my bail, I was again to have a domicile under lock and key until the new trial, unless my parent again put in an appearance upon the scene. But, even while the sheriff was preparing once more to escort me to jail, a voice from among the crowd in the Court-room sang out, in that delicious Irish brogue I had so often endeavored on the stage to imitate with my own tongue:

"Would yer honor accept the likes of bail, for the poor boy?"

It must be candidly admitted, that I had never before entertained so warm a love for the Irish brogue. It sounded like perfect music to my ears. Still more did it do so, when, after a brief confab between the Judge and the District Attorney, the proffered bail was accepted, and with a kindly but vigorous slap on my back, my new bondsman exclaimed:

"Now! my boy, all I ask of ye, is, that ye don't throw me in for the bail. When ye were shut up before, yer face didn't spake much for ye. But now, I couldn't bear to see a good-looking fellow as ye are trotting off to jail for nothing at all."

A roar of laughter from those who were present followed this speech. Very certainly, as my Irish friend said, my "face didn't spake much for me," upon that previous occasion, if it did possibly justify his warm-heartedness now. But, as the great dramatist says: "One touch of kindness makes the whole world kin;" and to a certain extent at any rate, on this occasion, it did so. His goodness of heart had struck an answering chord in the bosom of all the spectators. They crowded around me, offering their congratulations, and shaking my hands with a vigor which might have gone far to prove that they would have done the same kindness for me, provided they had merely chanced to think of it.

Once more, I returned to my father, and resided with him until the Court a third time convened, when I again returned to Waukegan, and proved to the goodhearted Irishman that the lad he had become bondsman for, was not "the boy to throw him in for the bail."

Now, however, I found that a change of *venue* had been obtained for the trial, and I was obliged to go to Chicago. It was a fourth time deferred, and on my inability or unwillingness to give new bonds in a city where I could easily have procured bail, I was ordered to prison for a third time. The sheriff, of course, had no discretion allowed him in obeying the order of the Court. He therefore conducted me to prison, when he duly locked the door of my cell upon me. Immediately after, he unlocked it, saying:

"Look here, Mose! I have obeyed orders and locked you up. Now I have unlocked the door, and am going to let you out, if you choose to act as my deputy."

Gladly enough, I consented and entered at once upon my duties. It would perhaps be unnecessary to say that the sheriff had a few years since contributed by his own patronage to my success as a pop-corn merchant, and had subsequently been acquainted with my theatrical struggles. In addition to this, he had heard the history of my connection with the case, and felt a kindly disposition to befriend one who had been unfairly implicated in the matter from the beginning.

CHAPTER II.

As a Detective—Hunting up a Horse and Buggy—A Runaway from the Sheriff—On the Track—The Hidden Corpse—Following the Murderer up—Struggle and Capture—Quick Justice—A Good "Utility" Man—Mosquitoes and an Old Steam-boiler—"How Rich you be"—Becoming a Rum-seller—What is in the Bone will out of the Flesh.

As his deputy, I endeavored conscientiously to answer the good opinion of the sheriff. Suffice it, I so far succeeded, that he recommended me very strongly to Pinkerton, the celebrated detective of Chicago. At this time, Pinkerton was going to Waukegan for the purpose of arranging the means with the authorities there for breaking up a gang of counterfeiters, then flooding the whole of Northern Illinois and Southern Wisconsin with bogus money. After a brief interview with me, Pinkerton appointed me upon his staff, and on his return from Waukegan, left me in that city.

Shortly after this, I received a telegram from my chief. It stated that a man, very gentlemanly in appearance (his description was given), had stolen a horse and buggy in Chicago. The fellow had gone northward, and Waukegan was designated as the place where he might probably fetch up.

When I received the despatch I was with the sheriff, and had just handed it to him, when an individual drove up with a horse and buggy, both of which closely answered Pinkerton's description. This person was hailed with the familiarity whose command is peculiar to the functionaries of the Law, and as politely, and with even more oppressive familiarity, requested to—

"Get out!"

The stranger was necessitated to obey this peremptory injunction, and requested information of its object in a blandly imperturbable manner.

"You are my prisoner," curtly responded the sheriff.

"For what, sir?" demanded the man.

"For stealing that horse and buggy."

"Good God!" was the instantaneous ejaculation. "You were never more mistaken in your life."

Certainly, the rascal would have made his fortune upon the stage, his look of astonishment was so perfect, while the touch of indignation in his manner heightened this appearance on his part so admirably. The sheriff looked at me as if in doubt. I nodded my head slightly. That which the fellow was only doing as an amateur, was within my professional experience.

"Yes, sir! you are the man," replied the sheriff.

"In a few minutes," said the stranger, "I will prove to you, you are the most mistaken man in the world."

"How?"

"Do you know Mr. Sutherland, sir?"

He had named one of the most prominent citizens in Waukegan.

"Very well, indeed!" was the response of the sheriff.

"Jump in my buggy, then, and we'll drive to his house. There, I can readily convince you, you are thoroughly mistaken."

"All right," ejaculated the sheriff.

In spite of my remonstrating look, he jumped into

the buggy, followed by the stranger, and they drove off.

It would be needless to detail my reflections. The reader, if gifted with a fair share of acumen, can readily determine them. In less than three-quarters of an hour the horse and buggy once more appeared, driven by the sheriff. He had been making the poor animal pay for his obtuseness.

"Well!" I inquiringly uttered.

"When we arrived at Sutherland's," said the local official, "the fellow got out and rang the bell. He was some time in waiting for the door to be opened. Then, he told me he would 'go round the house to the back door, and wake them up.' I waited some time longer, when the front door was opened by one of Mr. Sutherland's servants. Naturally enough, I got out, expecting to see the man within the house. Would you believe it, the rascal had never entered it."

"Very decidedly I should," was my exclamation.

Jumping into the buggy, I requested the sheriff, it is to be feared in a somewhat too dictatorial tone, to "lay it into the horse," and drive back. On arriving at Mr. Sutherland's, I asked him to indicate to me the way the man had gone. He could only point out the side of the house the runaway had passed round. Leaping out, I prepared to track him. It was then, that, for the first time in my life, I discovered, I possessed something of that sleuth-like certainty and readiness, which fitted me for portion of my future career.

The morning had been somewhat damp, and by the help of the print his feet had left upon a field at the back of Mr. Sutherland's dwelling, the fellow's track was distinctly visible for some half a mile. Here, the broken branches and twigs of a low hedge proved that he had crossed it into a lane. On the damp sandy gravel his track was even clearer. Then, he had encountered some one else, and near this spot traces of a recent struggle were apparent. From this point I could merely see one track, and was induced to believe there had been foul play, and that the fellow I was in chase of, had continued his flight alone. This led me to make a brief search in the neighborhood of the spot on which the scuffle had taken place. Just beyond the fence, roughly concealed by torn-up branches, lay the dead body of a man. The skull had been crushed in as if by the blow of a heavy club, and the pockets were turned inside out. I raised the arm of the corpse with ease. The muscles were limp and flaccid, not having had time to stiffen. It was evident that the murder had but recently been committed. My future trapper instinct was strong upon me, and I pursued the one trail for some mile and a half farther. There it was lost upon a stretch of higher and harder soil into which the lane had widened. Half an hour was spent in vainly trying to detect it, and then I made up my mind to return to the town, and give intelligence to the authorities that a murder had been committed.

After doing this, and reinforcing my somewhat jaded system with a draught of good Monongahela, I returned with the local police to the place where I had found the body.

On the way, I had made inquiries about the locality, and found that some half a mile beyond the spot where I had lost the trail, I should reach the main road, which led to Shiloh. Convinced now that the man was a determined ruffian, my young professional pride was aroused, and the determination was already formed by me to capture him.

Consequently, on reaching the scene of the murder, I left the authorities to convey the corpse to Waukegan, and recommenced my pursuit, making every possible inquiry at the houses and farms near the road, until I arrived at Shiloh. But I have neglected to state, that on my return to Waukegan I had disguised myself as thoroughly as possible, and placed in the pockets of my disguise a pair of darbies, (handcuffs) a revolver, and a brass-knuckle. The suspected murderer, and now known horse-thief, was a man of robust, almost of Herculean build. When recognized in the buggy, he had been dressed in the most fashionable style. Added to this, he had sported black flowing locks, with a dark and well-trimmed beard. He had now to be found in whatever other guise of dress or complexion he might choose to adopt, for the criminal *alias* of person or apparel is to the full as—perhaps even more variable than that of name.

My whole evening was passed in Shiloh, in wandering from one place of resort to another.

As yet, my search had been fruitless. But I never dreamt of failing in it, because I had determined to succeed. I felt certain, I should capture my man.

At last, I found myself in a beer-saloon, where, while standing at the bar and in the act of drinking, my eyes fell upon an individual whom I instinctively knew was the criminal I was in chase of. He had, however, undergone a great change. His beard was cropped, or rather it was shingled off short. As for his hair, it was notched and jagged, as if it had been curried with a comb that had razor-like teeth. His dress was by no means of that distinguished character which it had borne earlier in the day. This, however, arose more from the apparently slovenly fashion in which it was worn, than any other change in it.

It is true, he had been unable to alter his eyes, although, now, when he was off his guard, their glance was freer and more insolent than it had been when I had first seen him.

Besides, he had kept with him a cane which he had carried that morning. This was subsequently a damning proof against him, as the sheriff of Waukegan was able, as well as myself, to identify it.

When convinced beyond the possibility of doubt that this was the man, I quietly approached him, and dealt him a heavy blow with my brass-knuckles under the jaw.

This stretched him upon the floor. In a moment I was seated on his chest and his hands were secured and pinioned.

All had been effected so rapidly, that I was again upon my feet, before the by-standers had recovered from their surprise, and, it might almost seem, before the criminal could realize what had occurred.

The persons who had been so suddenly rendered mute by the rapidity of my assault upon the scoundrel, now found tongue. They approached me in an anything but friendly guise, demanding what all this meant, and why I had assaulted "Jackson" in this cowardly fashion. Only two or three, as I ought to mention, had given him this name, and these were decidedly the most disreputable-looking individuals present. Naturally enough, opening my coat, I displayed my official badge, and told them of the murder which the fellow had

"This stretched him on the floor. In a moment, I was seated on his chest, and his hands were secured and pinioned."—*Page* 30.

committed on the morning just passed, for plunder. The two or three I have alluded to as calling him by name, slunk out, while the rest, changing their tone, complimented me warmly upon the coolness and skill with which they were pleased to say the arrest had been made.

As for myself, I must own that when I looked at the thew and muscle of my prostrate captive, I was far more inclined to compliment myself upon the recklessness with which I had, single-handed, effected his capture.

Word was immediately despatched to the sheriff, and, by the following morning, Jackson was safely lodged in the jail at Waukegan, the county seat of Lake County. Shortly after this, he was indicted by the Grand Jury, and a change of *venue* having been granted, he was removed for trial to Chicago; where, pleading guilty, he was sentenced to be hanged, and paid the penalty of his crime upon the gallows.

As for my poor friend Lewis, he had already pleaded guilty to manslaughter, and been sentenced to imprisonment for eight years. He died before the term of his imprisonment had expired.

In those days, in the West, justice was far shorter and sharper than it has recently been in New York. There was more pride in the detection of crime, and considerably readier justice in its punishment. Red-handed murder had especially little chance of escaping the prompt retribution of the Law, and it will, I think, be granted by the inhabitants of the metropolis that the consequent fear was a tolerably fair degree of preservation for human life, considering the character of the various elements from which life in that portion of the States was then composed.

Having shortly after this returned to my home, I assumed the position of under-sheriff to my parent, and lived for several months somewhat quietly, being lionized in no small degree by my friends and neighbors on account of the capture of Jackson. In a few months, however, Pinkerton, who had evidently considered me a good "utility" man in the detective line, wanted my services again. He was engaged in ferreting out a gang of counterfeiters and horse-thieves, who had been circulating bad notes, and thinning out the stables above Chicago. Their base of operations had been made by them at the foot of Little Dalls, now called Dallton. This was some twenty miles above Portage City.

Excitement was the only thing I lacked while under my father's wing, and consequently, in spite of his remonstrances, I determined upon accepting the offer of employment which Pinkerton made me.

Starting at once, after seeing my chief, I joined the party with whom I was to work, at Madison. Here, after laying our plans, or rather, arranging for the execution of those Pinkerton had laid out for us, we separated, with the understanding that wherever we met, we were to proceed as if we had been strangers. The following day, myself and a companion found ourselves at Big Bull Falls. It would be unnecessary to trace out our after-route from place to place. For some time we discovered nothing which might afford any clue to the object of our search. At last we arrived at Grandfather Bull Falls, when something occurred which convinced us we had continued too far in that direction. We consequently returned, and took a straight line towards Black River Woods.

By the bye, the man who gave them this name must have had a hide tanned to the toughness of a leather boot, or he certainly never would have omitted to commemorate the plague of the mosquitoes which infest it.

Of all sections of the country populated with this delightful insect, that I have ever crossed, this is decidedly the worst. So much so, that I believe it must have been that part of it, in which the man we have heard of, took refuge from these winged atrocities under an old steam-boiler, amusing himself while in his fancied security by clamping their murderous beaks, with an old hammer he chanced to have with him, to the iron shell through which they were penetrating. The result of this style of proceeding was perfectly unforeseen by him. In some hour and a half, the muscle of the trapped mosquitoes was sufficiently strong for them to raise the iron shell and fly off with it.

Be this as it may, it is a complete purgatory. You, in vain, try to smash one mosquito whose fangs you feel in your forehead. While doing so, another fastens on your nose, and half a dozen more upon either cheek. The amount of profanity they caused on the tongue of myself and my companion, I even now look back upon, with considerable contrition.

The whole of this portion of the country, as far as Black River, was under Mosquito dominion; and when we quitted it, it was with the sincere hope, upon my part, that nothing might oblige me to revisit it.

When we once more met the balance of our party at Stevens Point, which had been as unsuccessful as ourselves in tracking out the game, it is now a question to me how our swollen and disfigured faces could be at all recognizable.

2*

After some consultation, it was decided that portion of the party should strike for the Little Eauclaire River, while another should go up the larger stream called the Big Eauclaire. Myself and companion remained for a few days at this place, and finding nothing determinate, dressed ourselves as raftsmen,—in red shirts and overalls, making up our minds to separate. Then, I hired myself out to run the Caughnaut Rapids, on a trip to Plover Portage.

It was on our way in return, when "gigging back," as the raftsmen term it, that I first caught a glimpse of success. One of the pilots, had to employ a term well used in the west and south of the States, "cottoned" to me. This was probably on account of my youth and apparent verdancy, as well as my muscle. I was just the sort of fellow he evidently supposed could be employed as a green hand in his illegal calling. We had been talking of the ways of living in the West one morning, when he said:

"Look here, young fellow, thar's many a way of making enough to live, that's easier than your'n is."

"How is that?"

"D' yer see this?"

At the same time he pulled out of his pocket a lot of "queer," or counterfeit bills. He must have had more than two hundred dollars of bogus money of different denominations—fives, threes, and twos—with him.

"How rich you be!" I ejaculated, with an innocent look of wonder.

"Do you think so?" he asked, with a sly wink and chuckle.

"Good Lord!" I cried out, as if the idea had just come to me. "They're not—"

"'D'yer see this?'"

"At the same time he pulled out of his pocket, a lot of 'queer' or counterfeit bills."—*Page* 34.

"Ya-as! They ar'—but don't make sich a row about seeing them."

As he said this, he glanced around as if he had been afraid somebody might have been within earshot of us.

"I only wish I could get hold of some of the blamed stuff."

"If yer do," replied he, "I'll introduce yer to them as makes it."

"Will you—re-eelly, do that?"

"Ya-as! young fellow, I will."

Accordingly, we started on the day after our return down the river, and having passed Dutchman's Rapids, entered upon what is called the jaws of the Little Dalls, at the Shingle. Thence, going by the Devil's Elbow and the Sag safely enough, we came out at the foot of the Dalls proper. Here my companion showed me the entrance to the cave in which the work of the gang was carried on.

He then told me I would have to wait at Portage City, until he could see his fellows in the business and obtain their permission to introduce a new recruit to them. Otherwise, it might be dangerous.

Afterwards, he himself returned to the neighborhood of the Sag.

While remaining at Portage, I met portions of my party, to whom I communicated the success I had met with. After talking the matter over with them, it was suggested by me that I should enter into the drinking-saloon business, which would not only afford me an apparent opportunity for disposing of the false money, but render it easy for me to bring my companions in contact with the counterfeiters. This was agreed upon, and when the pilot returned, I suggested it to him. He literally jumped at the idea, and ostensibly helped me in hunting up a location for my *début* in rum-selling, as well as vouching for me most strongly to the individual from whom I hired it. The rascal was well known in the place.

The whole of the time since I had arrived in Portage City, I was in constant correspondence with Pinkerton, who thoroughly approved of every step I was taking, and gave me to understand he would be ready at any moment to join me.

Well! my saloon was opened, and liquor-drinking was in full blast in it. The pilot was as good as his word. At different times, he brought down to me most of his accomplices, or rather of his employers, and I quickly became a sort of licensed favorite with them. Of course, if I had been detected in "shoving the queer," and found myself within the grasp of the law, they wouldn't have cared one red cent, but while I apparently bought their bogus notes, I was the best of fellows living. In the meantime, I had gradually introduced them to most of my companions, some of whom also took portion of their spurious money, paying for it in good cash. It must be admitted that the whole of the gang were capital judges of the genuineness of any of, or all, the currency of the various States. "Wild-cat" notes nothing could induce them to take in exchange, even for any of their own shinplasters.

Shortly after this, I found that the counterfeiters were to have a full meeting in the cave, which I had now several times visited. It was, I had reason to believe from what the pilot told me, for the purpose of dividing the spoils of the last month, which had been, so he hinted to me, unusually large.

My chief was immediately notified.

Very soon after, he joined me, with the United States Marshal, and made arrangements with the sheriff and city marshal to pounce upon the whole gang.

I say, he joined me. But this is scarcely the case, as he only saw me once previously to the night on which I knew they were to meet at the cave.

Arrangements, under his shrewd supervision, were capitally made. The cave had two entrances, one at the side of it, some considerable distance from the main one. A part of his men, with a section of the local police, under the United States and city marshals, were to be placed there to prevent any chance of escape. Himself and the sheriff of Portage were to be conducted by me to the main entrance. It would be needless to say, that as a desperate resistance to us was within the probable chances, every man in either party was well armed. Our suspicions respecting this were not, however, destined to be realized. Pinkerton's precautionary measures had been too well taken. When we were discovered, a rush had been made for the other entrance. Here, they found out that they had been completely trapped.

Then, rightly believing that the party at the main entrance was the principal one, they returned, and had a parley with the sheriff and Pinkerton, or rather with the last, ultimately coming out and surrendering.

After having been handcuffed, and placed in the boats, part of our men were left in the cave to secure the spoils, while the rest of us returned with our prisoners to Portage. It was one of the largest hauls of counterfeiters, with their implements of trade and spurious money, as well as a fair amount of good paper, which had up to that time ever been made in the West, and redounded very much to the credit of my chief, as well as myself—the last, mainly on account of the warm way in which he was pleased to compliment the share I had taken in it. Most certainly it resulted in the breaking up of the gang at that time known as the Guy Fox band, whose depredations had extended for several years from the Lakes to the Gulf. It had been the terror of the country, as it had resorted to every species of crime with the view of furthering their schemes. In due time they were all convicted and sent for various terms to the Penitentiary. All of them had the satisfaction of serving out their time, with one solitary exception. This was my friend the pilot of the raft, whose wish to make me a tool had led to their apprehension.

He was not, in every respect, a bad fellow, and his look of bewildered astonishment when, with the handcuffs on his hands, he saw me on the boat with Pinkerton, was so miserably pitiable, that I could not help feeling some tenderness towards him.

In the fulness of my heart, I spoke to my chief about him on the same night after our return to Portage.

"I will see about it, Mose," he replied, with a dry smile. "But, if you had as long an experience as I have, you would know how useless mercy would be to him. What is in the bone will out in the flesh."

The fellow was released, upon Pinkerton's application, some twelve months afterwards, and, as I have heard, verified my chief's appreciation of rascality. It has been said he was shot by a stalwart farmer, some three years afterwards, in the neighborhood of Dubuque, Iowa, in consequence of an attempt at highway robbery.

This fact, however, I am unable to verify. So, let my readers charitably hope, the lesson he had received bore the good fruit of turning him again into the paths of honesty.

CHAPTER III.

UNDER THE SHADOW OF MY OWN VINE AND FIG-TREE—TOO MUCH SYMPATHY—AGAIN IN THE THEATRE—MY FIRST TRIP ACROSS THE PLAINS—A FIDDLE AS A SENSATION—THE FREE FIGHT—MY FIRST LESSON IN SWIMMING—WANTED, A NEW BOW—JUDGMENT ON A WHISKEY-DRINKER—THE THIRD TIME—OUT HE GOES—A STAMPEDE—GROWING INTO FAVOR—THE HORSE-THIEVES—MILITARY JUDGMENT.

FOR a brief time, I again returned to my father, who had been unwilling that I should rejoin Pinkerton. He could stand my being deputy-sheriff under his own eye, but he did not relish my becoming a regular detective.

However, his term of office as sheriff was now expired, and I told him:

"I must do something."

"So you shall," he replied. "There is a nice little farm at some fifteen miles distant. I will buy it for you."

I had never yet resided under what Scripture calls "the shadow of my own vine and fig-tree." The idea struck me in a favorable light, and I cordially accepted his offer, although somewhat doubting my capacity in an agricultural line.

However, the die was cast, and in a few weeks I had settled down in the original occupation of our common parent, having at the same time become a married man.

It must be admitted that from the very start I found wedlock infinitely more agreeable than tilling the soil.

My previous almost nomadic style of existence had

to a great measure incapacitated me for this wearisomely primitive style of life. It was of no use trying to relish it. Luckily, there are all sorts of temperaments in this world, or what would humanity do for wheat, corn, and garden-stuff. My nature was decidedly not adapted to raising them.

My wife saw my utter incapability as a farmer. She was a good little soul, and frequently condoled with me on it.

This was the very worst thing, possibly, that she could have done. It added edge to my disgust with it. Night after night, when the day's work was over, were spent by me in querulously grumbling, and by her in consoling my discontent at my condition in life.

At length the farming season ended, and then my detestation of agriculture was doomed to be inconceivably heightened.

While I had out-of-door occupation, I could stand its regular monotony. Without it, what was there for me to do? I could but wander round the yard, and look at my pigs, fodder my cattle, take a stroll to the next farm, some three miles away, return to my little wife, expect her to console me, and then retire to bed, with the expectation of awaking to another day of the same humdrum existence.

My life had a necessity for positive activity.

The good little soul to whom I was married saw this; possibly too late. However this was, it came about that, with her full consent, although not without many tears on her part, and a considerable quantity of gloomy sorrow on mine, I left her at home, and struck out once more into the world.

It would be useless to narrate every incident of this

winter, but in the spring of 1855 I brought up at St. Joseph, Missouri.

Here, Maggie Mitchell was at this period playing as a "star," and to her I was indebted for a short engagement in the Theatre. It lasted for six weeks. When it came to a conclusion, I determined upon visiting California, at that time the Ophir and Golconda of the further side of this continent. However, it was no use starting with the small means I then had, unless some positive manner of living in San Francisco, at my first arrival there, was secured. Therefore, I telegraphed to Thomas McGuire, of McGuire's Opera House, who was about to open the New Metropolitan Theatre. In reply, he offered me an engagement for the September following. It was a long time to wait, but luckily I had recently become acquainted with John Crim, of the firm of Crim, Ebright and Coutts, who was organizing a party to cross the Plains.

He spoke to me about joining them, and in almost less time than it takes me to pen these few lines, I had arranged to accompany him.

It was upon the 6th of May, after having written a long and lovingly explanatory letter to my wife, I started from St. Joseph.

There were three hundred and seventy-five head of horses, and seventy-five men, all thoroughly armed and equipped. Each of them was furnished with a Sharp's carbine with sabre-bayonet, and a revolver. It was almost like the moving of a little army. The organization had been made in thorough military style, and perhaps with even more discipline, being under the command of Captain Crim himself.

Naturally, I was almost a total stranger to all of them

except our leader, but I soon began to form acquaintances, and in a few days became more especially linked in friendship with Dave Horner, the brother to Puss Horner, and the blacksmith of the party. The last was a sturdy Englishman, rejoicing in the *sobriquet*, by which he was commonly known amongst us, of Brighton Bill.

Our first halting-place was opposite Marysville, on the Big Blue River.

It then consisted of some four or five rough stone houses, covered with dirt, half a dozen *adobe* huts, as I have since learnt to call them, and a gambling hell, specially designed to pigeon emigrants in those delightful games known as Three-card Monte, the Strap Game, and others of an equally holy and pleasant character. This building, only of one story, was also the station at which the Pony Express changed horses.

After supper, Brighton Bill, Horner, and Pigeon—thus denominated because his outside attire was a swallow-tailed coat—strolled through Marysville. It was the first settlement we had struck since leaving St. Joseph, and we were curious about the customs, habits, and style of living of the place. In any case, I was so decidedly.

Dave had brought his violin with him. He was a capital fiddler, and in travelling across the plains, it is not always necessary to leave our business behind us. Dave certainly carried the means of displaying his accomplishment with him.

That fiddle created a veritable sensation. It might have been imagined that none of the inhabitants of Marysville had ever seen a fiddle before. His music was taken in exchange for whiskey, cigars, and anything else we wanted. Indeed, I began to believe that Captain Crim might run the risk of losing Horner as a member of the party. It almost seemed to me, as if, in a day or two, Dave might have become the owner of the whole settlement. However, in supposing this, I had not precisely calculated the full effects of temper and whiskey upon Brighton Bill. He began to feel the effects of the latter and by degrees lost the former. A somewhat scurrilously jocose allusion to his nationality was made by one of the natives. The indignant Briton no sooner heard it, than he struck out, right from the shoulder, in true Johnny Bull fashion. The offending native went down on the sandy soil of the High Street of Marysville as if he had been projected by a catapult.

Some few rows I had seen in my life before this, but never such a free fight as followed.

The whole of the male portion of the settlement (by the bye, it was nearly all of it) joined in the *mêlée*.

Had it not been for the assistance of many of our companions, who had also amused themselves with an exploring tour through Marysville, we might have got the worst of it. Luckily, they took a hand in the game, which saved us. Pistol-shots were, however, freely interchanged, and an individual was dropped, who had just drawn a bead upon Bill, with a bullet behind his ear.

After this, we retreated in as good order as we could, towards the river which lay between us and the spot where our camp was pitched.

The darkness of night had, however, by this time, fallen upon us, and being strangers, our party managed to become separated. Horner and myself kept together, but when we reached the stream, it was at a different portion of it from that where the skiff lay that had borne us over. We knew not which side to turn.

While standing there, we heard the sound of oars; or, more properly, of a means of propulsion bearing an equal consanguinity to oars and paddles. They were peculiar to the Plains at that time. What was to be done? If we had shouted to our friends, we should have disclosed our whereabouts to our enemies.

Horner, however, was a man of educational resource, and volunteered to swim across and return with the skiff for me, as I was unable to accompany him.

It may be imagined I felt some repugnance at being left to the mercy of Marysville, if it should chance to find me. Searching around, I stumbled over something, which, on examination, I discovered was an old "dugout," or species of impromptu ark. To this I at once determined upon committing myself and my fortunes, with a broad piece of board which I found at some little distance. This might serve as a paddle. Accordingly, as Horner plunged into the river, I availed myself of it. But the cursed thing gave me a lesson I have never since forgotten, when the chance was given me to remember it. It is contained in the old proverbial saying, "look before you leap." The dug-out had a hole in it. Scarcely had it got a dozen yards from the shore, than it was fast filling. In a few yards more, it was under water; and for the sake of remaining above its unpleasantly chilly surface, I, very considerately, let it go to—the bottom.

This was the worst fix I had yet found myself in.

But there is no lane without a turning, although it must be confessed some of these turnings are occasionally sharp and rough. Thinking my last moment was come, and that some time next morning my unconscious body might arrive on shore some miles lower down the river, to afford a meal to the stray dogs or crows of this part of the country, I struck out recklessly in a battle for as much more of life as I could possibly keep.

A few moments passed. Great Heaven! I did not sink. I was actually swimming.

"Where are you, Dave?" I shouted out, joyously.

"Here, old boy!" was the cheery answer.

That single exclamation settled my wish for conversation while in the Big Blue River. It had filled my mouth with water, and was very nearly on the point of bringing my first lesson in swimming to a most abrupt close. So I kept my tongue quiet, until at length I arrived drippingly joyous at the further side of the stream.

Horner was, necessarily, there before me, and assisted me to mount the bank.

"I thought, Mose, you told me you couldn't swim."

"Nor could I, Dave! You know, necessity is the mother of invention."

"So it seems," he dryly replied. "I only wish it would find me a new bow for my fiddle. The blackguards smashed that."

"It was lucky," I said, "they left you a whole skin."

"Upon my word! it was so," was his answer.

We then from the summit of the bank looked round us, and saw the welcome glow of our smouldering camp-fires, some half a mile below.

Horner spent the remainder of that night, after our return, in attending to his violin. The truth is, it needed it. I, however, slept soundly, and was awoke on the following morning at an early hour in very fair trim. The truth is, early experience had taught me what the results of bad whiskey are, and led me to refrain from an unhealthy indulgence in that exhilarating class of strong drink. But few of our companions had been as prudent. Brighton Bill and Dave more expressly felt the full effects of it; and with a parched tongue, and a splitting headache, heaped their fullest maledictions upon Marysville, and all the ungodly dwellers in that location, during the whole of that day.

His cold-water bath on the preceding night had, however, so modified the effects of whiskey upon Horner, that I was unprepared to find him so depraved in his appetite for it.

He was indifferent how he got it, whether clandestinely, to use the mildest possible phrase, or not. Happening to be on guard one night at our camping-place, he felt this thirst strong upon him. Not having the means of gratification with him, he actually bored a hole in one of the whiskey-barrels, and made free with its contents by means of a straw. In the morning he was what politeness would call "frightfully overcome." In good old Saxon, he was drunk.

Now Captain Crim had a holy horror of peculation —more especially, perhaps, of whiskey-peculation, when it was committed in the manner Dave had been guilty of. Nor in truth do I much blame him. Instead of boring the hole near the top of the barrel, and insuring himself merely sufficient, Horner had bored it about one-third down. He had also omitted to plug it up when he had satisfied himself. There was perhaps some reason for this, as when he had finished drinking he might have failed again to find the aperture.

At all events, when Captain Crim rose in the morning, one-third of the whiskey had dispersed itself over the bottom of the wagon devoted to its carriage, and

Horner's guilt was self-evident, putting his own state entirely out of the question.

A drum-head, or rather a whiskey-barrel, court-martial was immediately called together. The impenitent, because scarcely conscious, thief was arraigned, tried, and found guilty. Sentence was, however, suspended. This was partly, because, at the moment, he would have failed to comprehend its justice. More so, because it was hoped that when restored to complete consciousness, his friends might have influence enough with him to prevent the recurrence of so gross a breach of the laws of social equity. At first it appeared it would have done so. But again he fell from the high standard of morality on the Plains, and the captain had determined upon expelling him from the camp. Brighton Bill and myself headed the rest of the party in a strong remonstrance. At first Crim was disposed to defy us, but finding us all united in the wish to save the poor fellow, finally gave way.

The luckless Dave swore himself to perennial sobriety. But, alas! he once more fell from grace, in an emigrant-train. Then Captain Crim insisted with Spartan justice on the rigid execution of the lately postponed sentence.

What could be said upon his behalf? Those who had been willing to deal kindly with him upon the score of his fiddle, could find no word to urge in his favor. Possibly, in their eyes the liquor he had been guilty of abstracting was of greater present value, even, than his violin. One only of us stuck to him. This was a relative, I believe a nephew, of our captain.

"If you turn Dave out, you shall turn me, too;" he said pluckily.

Crim's lips whitened.

"Then, by the Lord!" he said. "Out you both go."

And out both did go, with such provisions as might be immediately necessary, horses, arms, and a sufficiency of powder and shot to last them until they were picked up by another train or scalped by the Indians. The last, however, I doubt, as although I never again heard of Dave Horner, I have reason to believe his companion is now settled in Sacramento, and is a prosperous merchant in that thriving city.

Until we arrived at Ash Hollow, on the south side of the North Platte, nothing of any moment occurred. Here as we were camping, a magnificent and noted bay horse, called Captain Fisher, took fright and started off at a furious pace with a number of the stock. In fact, it was a regular stampede, and one of the most exciting sights I had ever seen. However, I had no more than the first moment to enjoy it in. Action was a necessity, and my old circus-training stood me in good stead, to be of some service. I darted after the bay with a speed that nearly equalled his own. How long this would have held out, it is, of course, impossible for me to say. Something, however, caused Captain Fisher to swerve across my line of pursuit. Leaping, rather than running after him, I succeeded in grasping him by the rope attached to the hackamoor or halter. His terrified speed was so great that I was thrown upon the ground and dragged by him for a considerable distance. But for my long experience as a boy on the sawdust of the arena, it would have been absolutely useless for me to have attempted regaining my feet. How I escaped serious bodily injury from the remainder of the stampeded horses, I never knew. Escape I however did, as

3

well as again recover a standing or rather a running position. The rest of the business was now comparatively easy—indeed, a mere matter of time. Clinging to the rope, I compelled him to slacken his pace, until, at last, I succeeded in grasping the affrighted animal by the mane and vaulting upon his back. There, I was the master, and he was not long in finding it out.

It was about three miles from our halting-place when I succeeded in turning him. The remainder of the stampeded horses followed us. Thoroughly cowed by his past fright, and the certainty that he had to do as I chose, we arrived at the camp.

All my mates crowded round me with congratulations, and Captain Crim shook me by the hand as I leapt from the back of the other Captain with a warmth that was at the least as effective as it was affecting. It was the second time he had honored me. The first occasion was when I had entered upon my service with him in St. Joseph. Nor did his second grip mean nothing. It established me, with him, from that hour, as a prime favorite.

In the vicinity of Chimney Rock, we encountered an apparently agreeable party of some half-dozen travellers, who applied for permission to travel with our train. Captain Crim complied with their request, extending to them the camp privileges on condition of their complying with its necessary restrictions. Our new friends seemed not only grateful for his hospitable kindness, but too eager to display their gratitude.

They continued with us some two days, without exciting any suspicion.

During the second night after their admission to the camp, it happened to be my watch, and while on my rounds, I seemed to notice a movement in some of the animals which indicated that all was not perfectly as it should be. They did not seem as quiet as usual.

Bending closer to the earth and gazing along it, with my eyes covered by my hand from the glare of the camp-fires, I saw some description of animal, which I at once supposed was a coyote or Prairie-wolf. As yet, such an animal was unknown to me. To make assurance doubly sure, I raised my rifle to my shoulder, and in another instant should have blazed away at it, when it suddenly straightened itself up, yelling out frantically:

"For God's sake, don't shoot!"

"Come in, then," was my answer.

As the fellow gradually sneaked nearer to me, it seemed that I recognized him. And, very certainly, when he was within the light of the camp-fires, I did so. It was one of the party of agreeable gentlemen whom our captain had hospitably permitted to travel with us. The scoundrel had been tampering with the fastenings of our horses, preparatory to stealing them.

Never shall I forget Captain Crim's look of unutterable horror at the fellow, when I woke him up in his tent, with my prisoner. The indignation which he had exhibited on poor Dave Horner's third detection in whiskey-stealing, was nothing to it.

"A darned horse-thief! Who'd ever have thought it!"

"I assure you, Captain—"

"Hold your tongue, you infernal rascal, or, by Heaven! I'll make short work of you and your companions."

"Let me explain, my dear sir!" he whined.

"Have them all turned out, Mose!" thundered Crim.

"They are lucky to have me to deal with them. Any one else would have hanged the whole lot."

By this time, the whole camp was alive, more especially our forty-eight hour acquaintances. These disowned the culprit, as a stranger who had but recently joined them. Their defence was, however, too thin; and as the ominous murmur arose around them that—

"Lynching would be the shortest and best settlement of the matter"—

It was concluded by them, it would be wisest to obey. This, the more especially, as I had collected some dozen of my immediate friends, who stood ominously close to me, with rifles in hand, and six-shooters very palpably visible.

In another ten minutes, they had all left the camp.

When we arrived at Fort Laramie, Crim reported this gang of marauding horse-thieves to the officer in command of that post. Several days on our route beyond the fort, we were overtaken by the Pony Express, and learned that this very band had been captured in its immediate vicinity. Military justice is very prompt. It may make an occasional mistake, although not often. They had all been hung.

CHAPTER IV.

CAUGHT BY THE INDIANS—A PLEASANT RIDE—ONE PITYING FACE—BENEFIT OF BEING A MASON—THE EVIL EYE—INDIAN BEAUTY AND INDIAN EATING—THE OFFER OF MARRIAGE—DECLINING IT, MAKES ME A FRIEND—A SECOND AND MORE TEMPTING OFFER—DECLINING IT, DOES NOT MAKE ME AN ENEMY—PULLING UP MY STAKES WITH HONOR—THE PONY EXPRESS—AGAIN WITH THE TRAIN.

PREVIOUS to our reaching Fort Laramie, we had been able to procure plenty of fresh meat.

The antelope and buffalo had almost seemed waiting for our rifles. Now, however, we met with few or none of either of these, and the scarcity began to be severely felt.

Even Captain Crim grew more peppery with us than he had before been, and Brighton Bill lost his usual ruddy jollity.

Consequently, one morning, I started out with a determination to find fresh meat or die. To tell the truth, it came very near to being the latter.

As yet, all the Indians we had met with on the Plains had been of friendly tribes, and at this time no danger was anticipated. I was already some six or seven miles from our train, on the upper side of the North Platte, past what they call the Rattlesnake Hills, when I beheld approaching me a party of Indians. At this time, I was unaware what tribe they were, although now I should pretty readily be able to tell that they were Cheyennes. These are generally hostile to the whites, unless overawed by superior numbers. I necessarily mean, a proportionately superior number—about one, perhaps, to three. The party approached me in an apparently friendly manner, or else the fleet gelding I was mounted on might easily have distanced them. On approaching nearer, they requested, in the usual Indian manner, for tobacco or powder. The first, I readily enough gave them. The latter I was not inclined to part with. Suddenly one of the Indians drew closer to me, and laid his hand on my rifle. I pulled it back from him, and at the same moment was grasped round the waist from behind, by a savage whom I had not previously noticed.

My desperate struggles were in vain. I was torn from my horse, and in a few moments more found myself weaponless, with my arms pinioned behind me, and lashed on the back of one of their ponies. The raw hide-whangs round my waist were tied so tightly as almost to stop the circulation.

The animal was then turned loose, and followed with whoop and yell by the savages as if they had been nothing else than a band of devils. The Cheyenne who was probably their chief had appropriated my horse. How madly I wished that Charlie would throw the red demon as he galloped after me, shouting and whooping like an incarnate fiend.

In that mad race, for at the moment I almost fancied the Indians and myself were all lunatics on a wild race to the infernal regions, what a paroxysm of despairing thought rushed through my mind. Was I to go out of life something like the dying snuff of a candle, without one free blow in a square fight? And these were the Indians I had read of as a boy, these cowardly, sneaking red curs, who had not dared to give me a chance for my life. Great God! Where was Brighton Bill and my other companions? What would Captain Crim say if he ever heard of this? Then I thought of my father, Pinkerton, Maggie Mitchell; and, as my wife's face rose on my vision—my good little wife, I could or would think no more. All became momentarily a blank. Again, however, I returned to my senses. I heard the whooping yell of the red devil who was astride of my gelding, Charlie, and I cursed him in good round Saxon, as if he could understand me.

But what is the use of dwelling upon this. After a ride of some two hours and a half, in a fashion I had never expected to attempt, my captors came in sight of an Indian village.

Here I was cut loose from the pony upon which I had performed the most painful feat of horsemanship I had ever attempted, and dragged instead of led into the presence of the chief of the tribe. All the inhabitants of the village surrounded me. Squaws, old and young, papooses of either sex, and all the components of an Indian mob, were crowding around the white captive.

One only face I saw which displayed anything like pity. It was that of an Indian girl of some sixteen years. Whether it was pretty or ugly, I knew not. I only felt that I saw sorrow in her large and star-like eyes, as they gazed upon me.

Curiously enough, they gave me a sensation of hope. The moment before I had been madly desiring that the drama of life, with me, might come to an end. Now, I began to think and weigh my chances, which, to own up, at the present moment appeared slim enough for safety.

My hands and arms seemed almost dead, and some minutes elapsed before they recovered the consciousness of life. Looking in the face of the chief, I saw that he was an old man. As in great age it not unfrequently happens, his face had regained somewhat of the kindliness of youth. At any rate it lacked the repulsive character which marked that of my captor. Suddenly, it seemed to me—was I dreaming? No! This time, I was certain of it. He had made the Masonic sign of distress. The girl's sympathetic glance had been palpably an omen of good.

Trembling with agitation I responded.

What immediately followed I am unable to recall. Indeed, I doubt whether at the time I was thoroughly conscious of it.

When I undoubtedly had fully recovered my presence of mind, I found that matters had completely changed for me. The death at the stake, which had seemed to be my destiny, had faded from my senses. The red devils almost seemed to have been transmuted into copper-colored angels. I was seated on a buffalo-robe, and some of the older squaws were bathing my swollen limbs with cooling lotions, and looking—gratitude was almost compelling me to say what literal truth cannot. They certainly did not look in any wise amiable or handsome.

While this was going on, a tall and splendidly formed specimen of the red man entered the hut. He was dressed in a robe or tunic, magnificently embroidered with shells and beads. He had evidently been sent for by the chief, as I soon discovered, because he was able to speak English. The only blemish in his personal appearance was a sort of dip in his right eyebrow, which partially closed the organ beneath. White superstition might possibly have gifted him with the evil eye. The Indian name he bore somewhat corresponded with this, as he was called Par-a-wau, or "The Warning Devil."

First, addressing the chief (I afterwards found this was Old Spotted Tail) in their own tongue, he received an answer.

Then turning to me, he extended his hand and gave me the Masonic grip. After this, he seated himself beside me, and addressed me in my own tongue, asking how I came upon the hunting-grounds of the Cheyennes, where I was from, and whither I was going? When he had received my answers and repeated them to the chief in the tongue of their tribe, he next began to inquire very minutely about Masonry among the pale-faces. In subsequent conversations with him, for in the present case I had only to reply, I found that the Indians had first been initiated in its mysteries by the agents of the Hudson Bay Company. Neither had it been much carried beyond the northern and western tribes. This was learnt from Par-a-wau, when I began to feel perfectly at ease with him.

At this time I was merely a captive, although I had, from the mere chance of Old Spotted Tail's appreciation of my personal appearance, escaped the risk of no longer being one, by the most speedy means of escape from life my red acquaintances could have devised for me, consistently with their own amusement. Be it remembered, in stating this fact, individual vanity bears no part—the Indian idea of comeliness being very much the reverse, in general, of the white man's idea of that desirable qualification.

After his examination of me had been brought to an

end, he made an oration of some length to the aged Cheyenne chief. He had risen to his feet as he did so, and the grace of his movements, with his full and rollingly sonorous voice, might have done credit to the best of our own orators. Indeed, so completely did his gesture translate his speech, that I could almost follow every word of the appeal he was making for me. He was evidently pleading for my pardon. This I feel I should have received, if I am sufficiently a judge of human features to have translated the benign savageness of Old Spotted Tail's countenance. But there are always two sides to a question, and the young chief, who had appropriated not only myself but my gelding, Charlie, now put in for a long talk. I could swear he was not half as eloquent as Par-a-wau. However, what he said in a harsh voice, and with a large amount of what might be called temperate wrath, settled the question in discussion. The elders of the tribe gave him, twice or thrice, that discordant grunt of acquiescence which Fenimore Cooper, the modern writer, has translated more musically as—

" Ugh ! "

Consequently Old Spotted Tail pronounced a few words, and my red lawyer—so I began to consider Warning Devil, although I had been unable to fee him —turning to me, said in English :

"Will my brother come with Par-a-wau to his dwelling ? "

Of course I would, because I must. How, indeed, could I do otherwise ? So I followed him. The fact is, I had begun to entertain a certain degree of liking for the chief with the evil eye. He had befriended me. If my Cheyenne captivity had been a long one, I scarcely doubt that this liking would have ripened. However, I had now to accompany him. Let my readers conceive how great was my astonishment when I entered his hut after him, to find my first glance riveted by his daughter.

She was the Indian maiden whose look of sympathizing pity had, some two hours previously, called back my numbed senses to new life and hope.

"Will Clo-ke-ta provide my brother food?"

She too, then, spoke, or at any rate comprehended, my language, for she made no reply, but began to busy herself in preparing an Indian meal. During the time which elapsed before it was ready, I was able in a most satisfactory manner to take an inventory of her personal attractions. These I shall, however, refrain from inflicting upon my readers. Let it be sufficient to say that she was one of the most beautiful children of the red man (if not the only really beautiful one) I had ever seen.

Perhaps it was well for me, that while I was watching her every supple and graceful movement, the thought of the dear little wife who was waiting for me in the far East, appealed to my love for her.

Otherwise, it may have been possible that I might have forgotten civilization forever. The nomadic life had always great attractions for me. Where could I more thoroughly have indulged in it, than as the son-in-law of Warning Devil, and the owner of such a charming squaw as Clo-ke-ta might have proved to me? However, this was a wrong, as well as not altogether agreeable, reflection.

Turning my head with something like a sigh on my lips to Par-a-wau, I saw that his one unhidden eye was fixed steadily upon me.

"My brother is sad," he said. "But the trees are not always green. He must wait in peace until they once more bud."

He had scarcely interpreted the meaning of my sigh. Yet his poetical words (whatever nonsense may be prated about them by novelists, such Indians as I have met with rarely display any trace of poetical feeling) brought me thoroughly back to my present position, and I asked him:

"How long I should have to remain a captive with the Cheyennes?"

This he was unable to say, but he informed me Old Spotted Tail had granted me the freedom of the village, although with the precaution that an Indian guard should accompany me whenever Par-a-wau could not.

Clo-ke-ta now had the meal prepared, which was a very satisfactory spread for an appetite which had been unattended to since the early hour in which I left Captain Crim's camp. The jerked antelope and the roasted maize were in truth excellent, and if I only had been offered a horn of whiskey to wash it down with, I might not altogether have regretted the dinner I had lost. This, especially when I now remember the bright eyes and raven hair of her who attended to the need of my inner man.

The fancy, which Old Spotted Tail had evidently taken for me, was destined to exhibit itself in true Indian fashion.

He offered me one of his own daughters in marriage.

But I was not educated in Mormonism; and even had I been, it may be questionable, while I daily saw Clo-ke-ta, whether El-eu-e-na, which was the name of the chief's daughter, would have had any attractions for me. She was not particularly interesting in appearance. Whether she had any fancy for my luckless self or not, it would be impossible for me to say. An Indian girl's affections do not count for much in the eyes of their fathers. In spite of this, I most respectfully declined the alluring offer, through Par-a-wau, with, as he afterwards informed me, the most profound expression of thankfulness for the undeserved honor Old Spotted Tail had done me.

This seemed to me, as I listened without understanding, to greatly gratify the chief who had captured me, and led to a result that was infinitely more gratifying to myself, as he aspired to the honor of registering himself as one of Old Spotted Tail's sons-in-law.

On the same evening, however, I was destined to a really far greater temptation. It was after the evening meal, and I was seated near Par-a-wau. His child was putting away the willow platters and other means of serving up and disposing of the food she had, as customary, prepared. While she was attending to her domestic duties, Warning Devil, without any warning, addressed me.

"My brother has keen eyes."

"They are sharp enough at times, but they could not keep me out of the hands of the Cheyennes."

"He knows that El-eu-e-na is not fair to look on." I could not help laughing as he said this. "Nor would she make a good squaw. She could not prepare the buffalo or the antelope, nor clean my brother's rifle, nor embroider his moccasins, as a great chief needs that she should." What the deuce was he coming to? I was not doomed to wait long, for after a pause he addressed me this question in an affirmative manner, which I at once understood. "My brother has seen Clo-ke-ta?"

"Yes!"

"And what does he think of her?"

For my life, I could not have helped casting a swift glance at the Indian girl. She was standing near us, with her eyes veiled by their brown lids, and a crimson blush glowing through her dusky skin, over her cheeks, forehead, neck, and all of the upper portion of her person which was exposed. So fierily red was this flush, I could not help seeing it even in the gathering gloom.

"Cannot my father see with his own eyes," I replied. "She is as fair as the young red morning."

This was said by me in a grave and reserved tone, which among men of my own race would have precluded the continuance of the parent in what I felt he had been about to say. But I had not counted truly upon the Indian nature. My present gravity was the exact reproduction of his own. It was so unlike my usual manner, that he evidently supposed I had taken the matter he was about to propose into serious consideration. He consequently again spoke.

"If my brother will take Clo-ke-ta as his squaw, he shall be to Par-a-wau as a son, in place of the young warrior who is dead. He knows, for he has seen what Clo-ke-ta can do for her father's friend. She will do more for him who marries her. Shall it be as Par-a-wau says?"

It must frankly be admitted that for one moment the loveliness of the face I had just seen, and which I dared not again glance at, made me waver. Then, the memory of my wife and my own actual father rushed across

"Looking up, I told the noble savage, for I have the right to call him noble, all."—*Page* 63.

me with passionate force, and I spoke. I was no longer a coward.

Looking up, I told the noble savage—for I have the right to call him noble—all. I told him that I was already married, and had my father still living; that if I were to do what he had offered me the means of doing, I should bring a stain upon my name their tenderness might never blot from it.

For some time, all was silent.

Then I felt my hand clasped in the cold fingers of two small and dusky ones, and raised to the lips of Clo-ke-ta.

"My brother is right," she said. "If he made Clo-ke-ta his squaw, and left her to return to the East, Clo-ke-ta would die."

Immediately after, I and the Warning Devil were alone in the gloom.

It almost seemed to me as if Par-a-wau must have resented my implied refusal to marry his daughter. But he did not. Nay! on the contrary I soon found he either assisted me in my wish for liberation, or was glad to get rid of me. Nevertheless, I am inclined to think that my captor also assisted in promoting my liberation. In his wish to become the son-in-law of Old Spotted Tail, he was, at least, equally anxious to get rid of my presence in the tribe. On the ninth day of my captivity, the aged chief gave me permission to pick up my stakes and quit my enforced camping-ground.

In doing so, he presented me with many presents, among which was a war-club, magnificently decorated with Indian carvings. This, he informed me through Par-a-wau, would be a protection to me from all hostile tribes, east of the Rocky Mountains.

However, it was to the gratification of finding me no longer opposed to the chief who had captured me, that I was mostly indebted. This young brave restored me not only the gelding he had deprived me of, but my rifle, the revolver I carried, and even the tobacco-pouch which he had appropriated. Let no one, from this time, henceforth say that there is no gratitude in a savage breast. He had found that I did not propose standing in his way. Why should he interpose any obstacles to my removing myself completely out of it.

Par-a-wau also gave me a pony and a magnificent Indian robe or tunic. But the farewell that touched me most was that of Clo-ke-ta.

As I was about leaving the Cheyenne village, she placed in my hand, with a pair of embroidered moccasins, a flower. It was the one which among the Indians is supposed to typify memory and regret.

Regretfully, I looked after her as I left the Cheyenne settlement. She had, however, vanished. Only the Warning Devil and the young chief who had taken me prisoner, were visible among the thronging red men who were watching my departure. The last made a single gesture. It might have been interpreted to mean one of two things, either—

"God speed!" or—

"Please the devil! that I may never see you again!"

I was, at any rate, once more a free man, and had full liberty to wander where or in what direction I would.

The chief had given me two guides. As these Indians could not speak a word of English, I was in one sense of the word companionless. It was barely some two miles from the Cheyenne village when the wild waste of the country spread out in an unbroken plain before my view, and I almost seemed to feel alone in the world. The primal days of Adam seemed to have settled on the solitary waste. There was no friendly word to greet our progress, no hostile arm to impede our rushing gallop. Not the slightest sign of civilization was visible. The enforced taciturnity of the two Indians made this but the more obvious.

So, the first day passed.

On the second, I saw an antelope. The stillness, which had heretofore been unbroken by anything save the tramp of our animals, our own breath, or the muttered exclamations of my two guides, was now shattered by the crack of my rifle. As the antelope fell to the earth, I heard the guttural exclamations of my guides, in which they gave the expression of their wonder as well as their gratification.

It was very certainly a good shot. The antelope had been at long range. The two Indians had been astonished.

As they trotted off, to secure the fallen animal, I could not help feeling that in their eyes, at least, I had in some measure justified the benevolence towards me of Old Spotted Tail.

On the third day we struck the Emigrant trail. The night before, we had encamped in a spot which was as lovely as any I have ever seen. A running rivulet of deliciously cool water, fledged by green trees and arched in by the broad blue heaven, which girdles in life on the Plains, gave us, on its banks, a resting-place. Here, I slept well, and woke in the morning with a fresh consciousness of the life, vigor, and beauty of the world.

Two hours after our start this day, we struck the trail.

The guides came to a sudden halt, and pointing to the route I had to continue, abruptly left me. Their characteristic taciturnity had not deserted them for a single instant.

During the whole of this day I followed the trail, overtaking and passing one Emigrant train, from whom, naturally enough, I could learn nothing of any which had preceded it. On the succeeding morning, I, however, encountered the Pony Express, and on inquiry learnt that a long train, with a large number of horses, had been passed by it. This train had been encamped at Sweet Water, close to Independence Rock, near what the rider called the old Frenchman's.

"How far off, is it?" I asked.

"You may reach them or their halting-place by to-morrow noon," was the response.

He evidently did not know the speed of the animal I was mounted on, or my temper. It was before nine on the following morning, that I arrived at Captain Crim's halting-place. He had been detained here by a distemper which had attacked the horses, and possibly, as Brighton Bill asserted, by a faint hope that I might yet make my re-appearance.

The first who saw me approaching the camp was Tom Doyle. His wild shout startled all in the camp.

"Hillo! Here's Mose."

The cry was enough. In a few moments, I was surrounded and almost torn to pieces by the nervous hands which clutched mine. Even Captain Crim squeezed my fingers with his own stalwart grip, and told me, "how glad 'he' was to see me, whole and safe again."

After this came question and reply, so fast, that my tongue, silent during the last two days and a half, literally ached with its answers, and I was glad enough when the hour for eating came, to which portion of the antelope I had killed on the preceding day made no despicable addition, as game had still been scarce with the boys.

CHAPTER V.

A Tempest—The Brute with no Rheumatic Pity—An Impromptu Gallows—Hanging a Rascal—My Stage Wardrobe—Under Water with a Water-tight Wagon—The Keg of Whiskey—Its Unforeseen Results—A Mountain Cannon—Natural Soda-water—An Indian Attack—Raising my First Hair—Taking a Lesson from the Red Man—British Criticism—The Valley of a Thousand Springs.

The rest which had been given the horses partially restored them, and on the following day the train was again in motion.

After reaching what is known by the old Emigrants as the last crossing of the Sweet Water, Captain Crim decided to take a road farther north than the usual one. He had crossed the plains several times before. Knowing that the Sublett's route and Headspath Cut-off, as well as the Salt Lake line of travel, were peculiarly hard upon stock, he determined this time, to try a track of his own.

We therefore followed up the Sweet Water, crossing it repeatedly, and at length passed the Rocky Mountains. Thence we went to Green River.

This river presented us with great difficulties to find a place for passing it. The current is, at all times, swift and strong. On this occasion it was greatly swollen, in consequence of the heavy snows of the preceding winter, higher in the mountains. After hunting for an available ford more than half a day, one was at last discovered, and the horses were brought over without the slightest loss.

That night, however, we experienced a fearful storm, or rather a hurricane.

It was indeed such a tempest as I had never yet experienced. Neither has it had its parallel since in the whole records of the Storm Bureau established in Washington. The rain and hail descended in literal sheets of water and ice. The camp-fires were extinguished by their fury. Tents were torn down and the wagons containing our stores were flooded. The lightning blazed incessantly, and the thunder seemed to roll in one continuous peal.

Luckily for us, it was not of long duration. In some three hours it had spent its fury. Yet its effects were felt by some of us, for a length of time. Poor Pigeon especially was taken down by it with a severe attack of inflammatory rheumatism. Since his name was first mentioned, it has not again recurred. However, his sickness here forces him upon my notice in connection with another member of our party.

The next morning, all damage having been repaired, the train was again in motion.

Having passed the three Tetons, gigantic sentinels projected from the main range of mountains, we followed a little stream which Crim christened Pine Creek. Beyond this, we unexpectedly came upon a vast belt of snow, extending through the Wind River Range. With three companions, I went over it as far as Salt Creek. It was found to be completely impassable for the horses, averaging from six to twenty feet in depth.

After holding a council, Captain Crim decided upon striking directly south until we should reach Sublett's

Cut-off. Consequently we had to retrace our steps, and encamped some twenty miles down Pine Creek, for the purpose of doing that class of reconnoitering which is nothing else than exploring.

Here it is, that we have once more to do with Pigeon.

There was a man who had some interest in a small portion of the stock. For want of a better and less appropriate name, I may as well call him Rascall. While delayed in our enforced encampment, some of us were occupied in grazing the stock. Others were exploring in every direction for a means of crossing the belt of snow which hedged us in from our westerly route. Rascall had nothing to do. Poor Pigeon was lying in his wagon, as helpless from rheumatic pain as the train was in presence of its blockading impediment. Rascall, having no rheumatic pity, took advantage of the solitary and forlorn Pigeon, by ordering him out of the wagon. In vain did the poor devil remonstrate with him. He was utterly unable to move. Rascall determined upon proving this, and being alone with Pigeon in the camp, tried the common experiment of brutes, by thrashing him in the most unmerciful manner possible.

Like many other brutes, he did this without counting the possible consequences.

On the return of the boys to the camp, they heard of this from Pigeon, who was, from his harmless good temper, a general if somewhat despised favorite. Naturally enough, their contempt was forgotten in their pity. They determined upon a queer revenge for his treatment of poor Pigeon. They, consequently, rigged up an impromptu gallows by joining two wagon poles together. From this they suspended a full-length portrait of the offender, although, at first, serious thoughts had been entertained of suspending himself.

It would be needless to say that the likeness was scarcely of sufficient academic correctness to have justified its limner in claiming any position as a portrait-painter.

Seeing this, in order to avoid any mistakes, with the artist's permission, I inscribed beneath it "Rascal," in very unmistakable letters.

Either the portrait or the name had an immediate effect. Captain Crim, who certainly had an artistic eye for painting or printing, one or both, as well as an unmistakable love of justice, saw it. He immediately inquired into the matter, and then visited Pigeon. The poor fellow's statement was enough. As has been seen, Crim was not a man of many words, but of very decisive temper. He expelled Rascall from the camp, and it was only after some four or five days' wandering in its vicinity, and imploring any of us he chanced to meet for pardon, that on consultation with his boys the Captain finally allowed him to re-enter it.

At length, a way out of our difficulty was found. Through deep gorges and cañons we reached Lambert Creek, and after following it for some distance, crossed it, finding ourselves once more in the Green River region. Thence, striking across a lower range of mountains, we came to Sublett's Cut-off.

Shortly after this, above Ham's Fork an accident occurred to one of the wagons, which, although of slight account to the train, was of serious moment to myself.

In passing this stream, the wagon containing, with other property, the whole of my wardrobe, stage and otherwise, sprung a leak. It should be mentioned that wagons for crossing the Plains, are, for obvious reasons, generally made water-tight. Being struck by an undercurrent which rendered it impossible to move it rapidly, it foundered with all its contents. Seeing the mishap from the shore, our Captain sung out to the boys to save whatever of the unlive stock in it they could. However, without waiting for orders, I and Brighton Bill, whose personal property had gone under the water with mine, had both rushed to the scene of our loss, and entering the stream, were hard at work.

We remained in that wretched Fork for five hours, fishing out of it, as it seemed, everything but our own property. Necessarily, much besides this was lost. The infernal undertow of the stream carried all it could bear with it, away. Not only had it plundered me of my stage-wardrobe, but of the whole of my wearing apparel, exclusive of that I then stood upright in. Not even a single shirt was left me. At length, when it was evident no hope remained of finding it, sulkily angry, wet and chilled not only to the bone, but to my very marrow, I struggled, with the well-nigh as miserable Bill, to the farther bank. Here we found Captain Crim awaiting us. At his side, stood a consolatory keg of whiskey, and in his hand was the immortal tin-cup, so lovingly identified with daily life on the Plains, and the early history of our nation upon the Pacific coast. He was a sagaciously provident leader. Praiseworthily interested in our health, he supplied both of us with a liberal cupful of the fortifying elixir. Hungry, as well as cold, for it was now three o'clock in the afternoon, and I had eaten nothing since morning, I forgot my usual prudence, and asked him for another cupful of the inspiring fluid.

"Do you think you can stand it, Mose?" was his far from unnatural inquiry.

The whiskey had not yet sufficient time to put an end to the shivering produced by my protracted cold bath. My teeth were actually chattering in my head, with a castanet accompaniment to my discomfort.

"Certainly-a-a-a, I can-n-n-n, Cap!"

"The cup holds a good half-pint."

"And I have been-n-n-n in the water ha-a-a-lf a day, Captain!"

"Very well!" he replied, with a commiserating look at my drowned-rat-like appearance, "you shall have it."

He very certainly would never have allowed me to soak so much inwardly, had it not been for my thorough outward soaking. Nor, indeed, but for my tribulation under my recent loss, should I have desired such an inward soaking. As I swallowed the whiskey, I felt my whole frame bursting into a tingling and generous glow. However, nothing more is remembered by me until the following morning.

Then I awoke in Captain Crim's tent. I had been stripped to the skin and wrapped in a blanket.

My clothes, now, alas! my only suit, had been removed from my person by his orders, and dried at a large fire, whose smouldering embers were in the last stage of inanition without the tent. They were lying beside me. It was with a somewhat sheepish look, I imagine, that I got into them, for the Captain was already out and about. What blowing up might be in store for me from such a rigid disciplinarian as he was, I could scarcely imagine.

As I went, or to speak more truly, sneaked out into

the sharp morning air, what was my surprise to hear him say, in a cheery voice:

"Well, Mose! You are all right now, are you not? To work, my lad! I wish all my boys were like you and Bill! You worked yesterday, like a couple of heroes."

It was an agreeable reception, and so widely different from the one I had anticipated, that for the moment I forgot my loss. Straightening myself up, with a modest disclaimer of his praise, I resolved to keep my intended apology under the lock and key of a silent tongue.

It was, I think, about noon, some two weeks after this, we reached Bear River. Following its course until we came to Soda Springs, our camp was pitched for the night, between them and the silenced volcanic crater beyond.

This has been so often described, that to do so again would be a waste of words. But on a hunting trip some ten miles more or less North, I discovered another natural curiosity, to which I was the first to call attention. On entering a small valley, I heard a continuous whizzing and grumbling noise, which was unlike anything I had before listened to. Looking around, I saw in the scarped face of an almost perpendicular mountain a cavity some twenty-five or thirty feet above the level on which I was standing. From this cavity came a broad and persistent jet of steam. This evidently caused the sound which had startled me. It was the result of volcanic action of some description, although I was scarcely scientific enough, even in a small way, to reason this out.

Suddenly, without the slightest note of preparation, a

huge ball of hot mud and fragments of stone was projected across the valley from this opening in the precipice. It was followed by a sharp roar, like the report from some heavy piece of artillery.

As I stood watching the orifice from which the jet of steam poured for some twelve or thirteen minutes, this phenomenon was repeated, and in something more than an hour I counted some five repetitions of it.

Farther up the valley, which was about a hundred and fifty yards in width, according to a rough guess, I came to another curious phenomenon. Opposite this natural cannon, the valley formed a broad semicircle, and on the extreme side of this was a tolerably large plateau of hard and sandy soil, from the summit of which I heard a singular hissing sound. Hobbling my horse below, I climbed to the summit of this, and my curiosity was rewarded by the discovery of another freak of Nature. The summit of the plateau was surrounded with a number of funnel-shaped apertures, from which water constantly rose and fell again, bubbling and sparkling like the contents of a soda-water bottle after the cork has been removed. The taste of this water, which was warm, was, however, scarcely so agreeable as the temperance beverage to which I have compared it.

Slightly behind me, the natural cannon still continued to belch forth its projectiles from the scarp of the rocky fortalice in which they were stored. Here, perhaps, were a number of relief-valves which prevented its destruction by a wider and more devastating explosion.

There is naturally small marvel that on this day I killed no game. My time had been too much occupied in the examination of these singular exhibitions of created oddity, for me to track deer or buffalo, if indeed any were in the neighborhood.

For what reason I can scarcely say, the name I gave this place was Death's Head Valley. It retains it to the present day.

Our camp was broken up on the next morning, and we continued, in an almost westerly line, our course. We were advancing into a thickly inhabited Indian country. From time to time what we believed signals were given and answered from either side of the train. No Indians were, however, visible.

It became clear, when we encamped for the night by Raft River, that if the natives put in any show at all, it would be a hostile one.

The result of this was, that after our brief supper was over, Captain Crim detailed me to make a reconnoissance of the country round our camping-place. We had long since begun to employ military terms. The reconnoissance proved him to have been right. Low and partially smothered Indian fires were detected by me, through the smoke rising from them, upon every side, and on my report being made, our guards for the night were doubled.

Next day, by its events, amply proved the advisability of this vigilance.

We had reached the City of Rocks, some seven or eight miles from the point at which we had crossed the last-mentioned stream. The advanced guard under me were moving cautiously along, exploring, almost, I had said, every inch of the road, and occasionally throwing a quick and marvellous glance at the springing spires, stretching battlements, cupolas and towers which bore witness to the plentiful imagination of the great Primal Architect and Supreme Master Mason of the earth, when we began to discover visible traces of Indian life. Some ten minutes after, the whole of this strange city of the unliving was literally blackened by live and threatening red-skins. The word, inappropriate as it may be to their color, must be pardoned. There was, and consequently is, no more time to pick phrases than to indulge in any descriptive power I may possess.

Giving the alarm, we fell back on the main body of our party.

Never before had I so much occasion afforded me to admire the natural nerve and military capacity of our leader, in a position of emergency.

The wagons of the train were formed in a close circle, with the horses hobbled inside, so as to prevent the chance of a stampede.

As for ourselves, we were posted under cover of our improvised fortification, to await the attack, which was not long before it burst upon us.

These preparations had been as speedily made, as the orders had been readily given.

They did not take the boys more than ten minutes. Nor had we been any too rapid in perfecting them.

A description of the fight would be impossible for me, as I only could detail that portion of it in which I was bodily concerned. It may be sufficient to say, that the first pitched battle with the red man, in which I was concerned, lasted for perhaps some fifteen minutes. The savages then seemed to have enough of it, and retired in admirable disorder. The right term would possibly be this—they ran away.

Dashing out after them, we followed the flying red-skins for some distance, and I had the satisfaction of raising my first hair, or in the language of the East, taking my first scalp.

An Indian, who concealed himself behind a large rock, discharged four arrows at me almost with the continuous rapidity of the lightning in the tempest we had so recently experienced. But what might be good for the goose might be equally good for the gander. Rocks were at a fairly large discount in that city of them. Taking advantage of one of these, I seized the opportunity afforded me by an unguarded movement of the enemy and dropped him with a bullet through his brain.

Some three more dead Indians lay scattered round the wagons, while only one of our men had received any hurt. He was an Irishman, who had received a shot in the right side. It had been made with a ragged ball, which had torn his flesh frightfully. However, the wound did not prove fatal.

The City of Rocks was now quiet enough, and shortly after Captain Crim gave orders for again starting.

Very necessarily, we were too fully employed in discussing our first Indian fight (or more properly perhaps I was, as several of my companions had crossed the Plains before) to indulge in a prolonged examination of the quaint, natural architecture through which we were moving.

On arriving at sundown near Goose Creek, our captain decided upon an extended examination of the country round, before entering the cañon. His reason for this was, that, on two previous occasions, the Indians had in this locality robbed him of all his horses, leaving him to find his way to California on foot. Little wisdom exceeds that which is taught us by past misfortune. At least, I may safely swear that I have generally found this to be the case.

Our men were accordingly divided into three parties, of tolerably equal numbers.

One had the care of the train and horses. Another had to pass across the mountains on the right, and the last, those on the left of the cañon. Crim did me the honor of detailing me in command of the second party, because his past experience had convinced him this was the side from which most danger might be expected, and as he was pleased to observe, I "had not only pluck enough for anything, but plenty of prudence." In the first part of this compliment, I completely justify his eulogy. The second portion of it may be subject to more question, especially when my youth is remembered.

My party consisted of twenty-eight of the best men connected with the train, amongst whom were Brighton Bill.

Some three miles along the side of the cañon we began to move in regular Indian fashion, singly and as quietly as we could, availing ourselves of every cover possible. Neither was this one whit too soon. As we crept over a small hill, we discovered, not more than six hundred yards from us, a party of red-skins. These were some fifty in number.

Luckily, perhaps, I had been the first of my party. Dropping as if I had been picked off by a bullet, I motioned my men to imitate me.

Then, placing my finger on my lips with a warning movement, we began crawling to the right, behind a number of huge rocks, and managed to advance to within some two hundred yards of them, without giving them the slightest alarm. The red devils were watching the movement of the train as, below them, it wound slowly up the cañon. More than probably, if they could count the number of boys we had left with it, they were congratulating themselves on the way, in which they must have supposed, they had thinned us out.

Raising my rifle I took deliberate aim, in which I was imitated by the rest of my party. Each of us had selected his own man.

The report of my weapon was followed simultaneously almost by the whole of those of my fellows, ringing out sharply and clearly.

As the smoke cleared away immediately after, we saw the whole of the Indians, who had not been slain, flying at the top of their speed across the mountain.

Twenty-three of them were on the ground, dying or dead, of which five were undoubtedly white men. Brighton Bill gazed upon the dead bodies reflectively.

"You're as good as an Injin, Mose!" he said. "But look 'ere. Wouldn't it 'ave been better to give 'em the lead, face to face."

"D' yer think the skulking beasts would ha' given yer a fair chance?"

This was said by one of the most silent men, and best shots, who had enlisted with Captain Crim.

"That's so, for sartain!" cried one of my boys, with an oath.

"I jist tell yer, Cap!" said the man who had replied to Brighton Bill, as he kicked over one of the dead bodies in which a ball had perforated the skull—probably it was that of the Indian he had drawn a bead on, "this was a darned square bit of Injin cunning.

·Yer've shown 'em, two can play their game. I'm proud to sarve under yer."

Brighton Bill said no more.

He was evidently thinking profoundly upon the different style in which matters were managed in crossing the Plains, to that in which they might have been, in case of necessity, in his own country.

On rejoining the train at the head of the cañon, and reporting the affair to our Captain, he was pleased to say, I had proved the justice of what he had said, when he appointed me to the command of the party. The congratulations on my success, however, which I received from my companions, were considerably warmer and more gratifying. For some twenty-four hours, I actually found myself promoted by general acclamation to the position of a hero. A little pluck and caution count heavily on the Plains.

Bill, however, did not change his opinions. Although still as warmly as ever attached to me, he said on the same evening, while sitting round our camp-fire:

"I don't care, Mose! It would 'ave been more square to give 'em the lead, face to face."

Late on the following day we reached Thousand Spring Valley, where the head-waters of the Humboldt River take their rise. Here water and game were good and abundant, and the train remained two days to rest the stock, while I and some others scoured the adjacent country in quest of fresh meat.

A lovelier spot than this valley, it would, perhaps, be impossible to find in the whole continent, and I could, while I wandered through it, scarcely avoid reflecting on the change which a hundred, or in all probability no more than fifty, years might produce here. Then, it will be thoroughly peopled. Possibly, a great inland city may have been reared by the bustling and intelligent life of my country. The red man will have been effaced by the onward march of civilization, or compelled by sheer necessity to accept a settled life. A Sharp's rifle or a colt will no longer be possessions of paramount necessity to him who travels thitherward. The buffalo will have been cleared out from this section of the States, and an antelope steak will be a rarity. At that period a man of my, at this time, nomadic instincts will be compelled to search for fresh ground in which to develop and enjoy them. The interior of Africa or South America will be the only parts of the world in which he can follow the life of a wanderer, unchecked and unhindered.

CHAPTER VI.

THE MISTY MORNING—ANOTHER INDIAN SCRIMMAGE—MOUNTAIN-FEVER—NEVER SAY DIE—A RASCALLY PROCEEDING—MY SIX-SHOOTER AND A SOMERSAULT—"LO! THE POOR INDIAN!"—HIS LETTER OF INTRODUCTION—THE ULTIMATE WARMTH OF HIS RECEPTION—NEARLY SQUARING ACCOUNTS—A RELAPSE—LEFT BEHIND IN HIGHLY DRAMATIC ATTIRE—FIRST RESULTS WITH NEW ACQUAINTANCES—KINDNESS OF MY CAPTAIN—GREATER KINDNESS OF HIS FRIEND—BECOMING A GOLD-DIGGER.

It was what sailors term a nasty day when we left this valley. A heavy mist, which was almost rain, veiled the surrounding range of country. Little beyond the eighth of a mile, in front of us or on either side, was visible.

About noon, some of our scouts brought the Captain information that matters looked squally, ahead of the train.

In fact, they had discovered some fresh traces of our red enemies. A halt was at once ordered, and I was despatched ahead with forty of the men to discover, if possible, what the present danger might be.

Nothing for some time presenting itself to verify the report Captain Crim had received, I took a leaf from his book and divided my boys into two parties. This resulted about half a mile farther in a sharp firing from the other party, which suddenly ceased, and in a few minutes more we came across the Indians, who were retreating in good order. Once more, I turned what I had learnt since I first joined Crim, to good account. Concealing my men, we astonished them by a round volley, which sent them off in double-quick time.

We were once more masters of the situation, and shortly after the train was again advancing.

Keeping a careful look-out, in order to prevent an ambush, this evening we struck Gravelly Ford, on the southern bank of the Humboldt.

After we had crossed this, I was taken sick with that terrible disease, emigrants have named the mountain-fever. For the last two days, I had been feeling somewhat under the weather, with occasional racking pain and headache. Never having previously known what actual sickness was, save from the result of accident, I had fancied it was nothing, and would speedily pass away. But, I was wrong. Unable either to walk or ride, my companions were obliged to place me in a wagon, and I became an invalid under the charge of the doctor who had accompanied us.

Captain Crim was more than kind to me at this time. In fact, he would not give me up, although the doctor, ignorant of the toughness of my constitution, actually told him that I was past recovery.

"We'll never say die, doctor, until we leave him behind us, with a wooden board at his head."

It was impossible for me to avoid hearing this, as the observation was made by Crim at a few yards' distance from the head of the wagon in which I was stretched. In spite of the pain and thirst from which I was suffering, as well as my exhausted condition, I could not refrain from a hollow chuckle, knowing how much life there was yet in my body. At the same time, I could not but feel grateful to the Captain for his words. It was clear he did not intend my bones to be cleaned by a stray wolf or some carrion-devouring bird, whose scent might lead them to my carcass.

But I did not know how the villany of one man was watching for the chance of putting me out of the way.

My protection of poor Pigeon had made me an enemy in Rascall. He had heard what the doctor said, and went among the men, some of whom detested me on the score of the favor the Captain had accorded me, grumbling over the necessity of carrying "deadweight!" In this kindly manner, he had disposed of me before I was fit for burial.

Through this fellow's instrumentality, I was, when the Captain happened to be at the head of the train, taken out of the wagon, and placed upon the earth, wrapped in a couple of blankets, with a small quantity of water beside me.

At this time, I was too weak even to utter a feeble remonstrance.

By a fortuitous circumstance, or I should possibly say a providential one, Brighton Bill came by shortly afterwards. In his astonishment he approached and spoke to me. I was utterly unable to make any reply. My friend—for in spite of his opinion in regard to my manner of settling accounts with the Indians, he proved himself a true one—hurried on to the Captain, whom he reached some quarter of an hour afterwards.

His rage, as well as that of most of my companions, was, as Bill subsequently told me, frightful. He grew absolutely livid with wrath, ordering an immediate halt, and coming back himself, to superintend my removal from my present couch to the wagon Rascall had taken me from.

"We'd better string this Rascall up, at once. He's a dirty varmint, and not worth shot or powder."

This was the expression of opinion of the silent individual, who had declared his gratification at "sarving under me." It would have been put in execution, there can be small doubt, if Captain Crim had not chanced to hear it. Nor, do I think he would deeply have grieved over this way of settling matters between me and Rascall. However, the position of the latter with regard to the cattle which has been earlier stated, prevented Crim's having any ostensible hand in such a condign punishment. He consequently suppressed this inclination on the part of my companions, giving the fellow, who for several hours kept out of his way, a severe reprimand, and adding a significant hint, that should I chance to recover, it would be well for him if he gave me a wide berth in future.

Singularly enough, from the hour in which Rascall had calculated to leave me behind the train—like a worn-out dog kicked from the door of a brutal master's dwelling—I began slowly to recover.

One might have supposed that the lesson he had received, in the way his conduct had been met with, both by the boys and our Captain, might have prevented any further exhibition of his dislike to me. However, this was not so. Some two days after, while I was still too weak to leave the wagon, he seized the opportunity of its being comparatively alone, to order me in an insolent manner to—

"Get out of it, and walk."

As I gave him no answer, he jumped into it for the purpose of beating me, doubtless, as he had formerly treated Pigeon. While his hand was lifted, however, he found himself covered with my six-shooter. Although too weak to walk, I was now strong enough to have pulled a trigger, and he saw I was.

"You had better get out of this, you infernal scoundrel! unless you prefer a bullet in your body."

Low and weak as my voice was, it was determined enough, to rid me of Rascall's presence. The way in which he vanished was so rapid, that had I been in a condition for it, one of my old peals of laughter would have accompanied the somersault with which his retreat from the wagon was effected.

We had reached Smoke Creek before I was enabled to rise and crawl, rather than walk, for the first time through the camp. Here we passed two days, only relieved by an attempt, on the part of the Indians, to stampede our stock. It seemed to me as if this attempt had settled the fact of my recovery. At any rate, I found myself again able to use my rifle with something of my old vitality.

Then we passed to Mud Springs, where we again rested for two days, the feed for the cattle being excellent.

From this place, our track was one of the meanest ever fashioned by God or man. Rough fragments of rock, deep gullies, rapid descents, and almost perpendicular rises, with occasional quagmires and tangled grease-wood, barred the road. We had to move over the ground with as great hesitation and caution as a fair dame displayed in navigating Broadway, during the snows of the last winter. It was possibly in the very worst part of this diabolical track, that we were confronted, as if by magic, with a red-skin.

He made signs of peace, and on being permitted to

advance, presented Captain Crim with a paper from the Indian agent at Pyramid Lake. This Indian agent, like all the others of the class employed by our Government, was undoubtedly as little acquainted with the nature of the red man as any Member of Congress could well be. Phil Sheridan understands him a good deal better. Well, this document set forth that the bearer was a good Lo, and friendly disposed, recommending any emigrant-train who might encounter him, to give him biscuit, bread, tobacco, or any other such luxuries in their power to bestow. Of course, I do not vouch for the exact words of this precious paper.

Our Captain complied with the half-request and half-order, and the Lo left us.

Scarcely had we advanced a mile farther, than he appeared again at the head of our train, in the company of thirty or forty other Los, all mounted on the regular Indian pony. Let me here say, that a dirtier and filthier set of red-skins, I never saw. Had the wind set in our direction, I feel the perfume exhaled from their carcasses would have been overpowering. Once more displaying the paper he had before shown, they again commenced begging. More provisions were given them by Crim. Actually loaded down with bread, corned meat, flour, sugar, and other dainties adapted to tickle the aboriginal palate, they at last departed.

"Did you see, Cap!" I asked, "how, the red beggar to the right of the fellow was eying our horses?"

"Yes! We shall have a little trouble before long."

"Good Heavens! Then, why did you give the stinking devils what they asked for?"

"You see, Mose, the scoundrels showed me that worthless paper. To be sure, I might have done what many would, and peppered them at once. It would have saved us a few hours' time and trouble. However, if we have to go in for them, there will be some satisfaction in knowing it is entirely their own fault."

"Do you not see they have stopped at the turn of the darned track, Captain?"

"Yes, Mose, I do."

"You do not mean to give the thieving vagabonds, anything more?"

"Certainly I do, Mose." He said this, grimly fingering his rifle in an ominous manner. "But—"

"Well, Cap!"

"Look here. Just leave the vagabond who showed us the agent's dirty hieroglyphic, to me."

In another instant, yelling like demons, the Los dashed upon our line. By accident, it may be presumed, Captain Crim's rifle, with mine and a dozen others, were discharged; and in five minutes more not a living red-skin was to be seen, on either side or in front of us. In a country traversed by a road like this, pursuit was of course vain, although it was attempted.

It ought, however, to be here stated that, until this occasion, I never knew what a capital shot our leader was. He was essentially a modest man. Nevertheless, his bullet had crushed through the skull of Lo, "the poor Indian," immediately above his left eye.

Towards night we pitched our camp at the lower end of Honey Lake Valley, some three miles from the entrance of Susan River into the lake. Continuing from this spot for two days, towards the small town of Susanville, and fording the river with our horses, we turned them out to graze for the balance of the day.

It was while seated under a large cottonwood tree, with four or five of the boys, watching our stock, that I nearly squared accounts with Rascall. No apparent remains of the mountain-fever forced me to rest in the wagon at the close of a day's ride, and having crossed the stream with them, while keeping a watch upon the horses, I was indulging in the first hour or two's free conversation I had with any of them, for some time. Suddenly, Brighton Bill, who had hitherto remained silent, looked up.

"'Ow was hit, Mose?"

"How was what?" I inquiringly demanded from him.

"Why, 'ow was hit that villin Rascall didn't thrash you, as 'e did Pigeon, when 'e got hinto your wagon?"

As I was relating a somewhat ludicrously-exaggerated account of the somersault performed by him, when he saw my six-shooter peeping out from beneath the covering blanket, Rascall, who had crept up behind the tree under whose branches we were sitting, roared out with savage vehemence:

"You're a lying son of a ——"

No sooner had the blackguardly epithet left his lips, than I was on my feet. My pistol was at once in my hand, and I fired.

Fortunately for him, as I did so, Bill struck up my hand, and the ball passed over his head. The cowardly ruffian took to his heels, very much as if he fancied the devil himself was after him.

We afterwards found that he skulked round the town. Nor did he join the train again until it reached Mountain Meadows. If I can fairly estimate a man's thoughts by the expression of his face, I should candidly say that

Captain Crim's features betrayed as little pleasure at seeing him again, as I undoubtedly felt. He had necessarily heard of this occurrence, although he never in any way alluded to it, when chancing to speak with me.

The natural excitement of this affair caused a relapse, and it became apparent that I must have some positive rest from the wear and tear of the journey. It was consequently decided that I should remain at Roop's Ranche, when we reached that place. With great kindness, Brighton Bill decided upon accompanying me there.

But at this time, the only suit of clothes I possessed were those I stood up in, and these had been, by travel, hardship, and exposure, reduced to so thoroughly a dilapidated condition, that each separate garment barely held together. In addition to this, they were worn out both at the knees and elbows. While I was disconsolately thinking of this, Bill had been occupied in looking through the various wagons. Suddenly I heard my name pealing joyously from his lips.

"Hi! Mose. Look 'ere!"

Yes! It was, unequivocally, a carpet-bag which belonged to me. My theatrical wardrobe had departed from me. Very probably this precious waif from my baggage contained all that I needed. Judge what my disgust must have been, when, on opening it, I drew forth one pair of corduroy knee-breeches, a scarlet waistcoat, and a long frieze coat. It was nothing, more nor less, than the complete stage costume of an Irish peasant, which I now remembered having stowed away in the carpet-bag, for the sake of packing my more reputable daily clothes where they might lie flat, without the chance of creasing more than necessary.

I was too weak to swear, and far too depressed in spirit even to grumble. These clothes were, at any rate, sound and whole. This was a point in their favor. So I decided upon wearing them.

On finding myself at the ranche, I was a decided object of curiosity and jeering comment to those with whom I was about to make my temporary home. Having very little money, and being still too weak to work, the immediate prospect was by no means a cheering one. While I was gazing round me, Governor Roop came by, and seized with no unnatural wonder at the unusual clothes of the new inhabitant, paused to question me. Had I been in good health at the time, it may be presumed that my tongue would readily have found words. Now, my teeth seemed to stick together, and my lips could not move. It appeared to me I was like some sailor stranded upon a strange shore, without any help, among treacherous and jeeringly inhospitable natives.

As this thought crossed me, a kindly hand was laid upon my shoulder, and a cheery voice cried out:

"My boy! you surely did not think I had forgotten you?"

It was Captain Crim who spoke. He had ridden into the town for the express purpose of recommending me to Governor Roop, with whom he was an old acquaintance. It would be useless, as well as a gross piece of vanity, were I here to relate all my late leader said of me. It will be enough to state here, his words were more than enough. The Governor gave him his ready assurance that I should want for nothing, until my former health and energy were completely restored.

Then, turning to me, he bade me follow him. On

"On finding myself at the ranche, I was a decided object of curiosity and jeering comment to those with whom I was about to make my temporary home.—*Page* 92.

arriving at the only hotel in the place, he told the landlord to give me the best room in the house, and allow me to remain as long as I desired. The account was to be charged to himself.

It would be impossible for me to keep my engagement in San Francisco, on the tenth of the coming September. Indeed, I had requested Captain Crim, before quitting the train, to explain this to McGuire. As for my dear little wife, to whom I had written so hopefully from St. Joseph, what could I now say to her? I dared not write. In spite of Crim's kindness, and the even greater kindness of the Governor to a perfect stranger, that afternoon and evening were passed by me in a condition of extreme depression.

With the next morning, a happier state of mind came. For the first time in many weeks, I had slept in a decent bed. It was certainly not a palatial hotel, yet my breakfast was a better one, as well as more approximating to civilization, than any I had recently enjoyed. The sun shone through the curtainless windows in an inspiring way. The movement of the life around me was different from that which I had recently experienced. In fact, all, for the time, seemed new. The complete change had already comparatively reinvigorated me.

From this moment I began rapidly to recover my health, and in a few weeks was able to look around for such employment as the place could afford.

Nothing available could be found.

During this period, I had frequently met with miners and conversed with them. The chances and struggles of their life had a considerable attraction for me. At last I decided upon "prospecting" for gold. Success in this appeared to offer me the only possibility I could see of repaying Governor Roop what I had cost him (his kindness to me it would be impossible to repay) and leaving the ranche, like an honest man. After spending some two weeks with little or no success, I, at length, established what I believed to be a good claim in Light's Cañon.

Honestly, I may say that I went to work with a will. Fortune, however, was long in coming. For many weeks, I made merely enough from my claim to whet my appetite for more.

Perseverance however generally pays. At last I made more than enough to pay my debts. A few days after accomplishing this, I had cancelled my debt to him who had so kindly befriended me. Then, as the winter had begun somewhat earlier than usual, with many thanks to the Governor, I located in Susanville, where I decided to remain until the spring.

The truth is, I had already tasted the keenest excitement I had yet found in life, because it is the most fluctuating and uncertain. The chances in gold-prospecting and gold-digging are so variable, that I defy any young man who has once tempted them, readily to put them from him. The poor devil who has been at it for months, and gained merely enough to sustain his existence, may, in a single afternoon, find his toil munificently rewarded. Like the gambler, he stakes. It is not money, so much as life and work. A single hour may possibly give him a thousand-fold the value of that which he, perchance, considers an almost worthless stake.

CHAPTER VII.

AFTER GOLD—THE PAH-UTE AND WASHO INDIANS—RUNNING OFF STOCK—PAYING TRIBUTE—THE OATH OF VENGEANCE—SOME SILVER BULLETS—"KNOWING DEM VELLERS"—AN UNGIRTHED SADDLE—THE UNBALANCED ACCOUNT—RECRUITING—THE BUCKSKIN RANGERS—A LITTLE BIOGRAPHY—MY NEW HORSE—A STORM IN THE MOUNTAINS—UNINTENTIONAL FIRING—OUT OF THE TEMPEST.

IT is unnecessary for me to detail the events of my campaign for gold during the following year and a half. At this moment, wealth seemed within my grasp, and in the next I might be mourning over or cursing my unrealized hopes. However, in 1857, wearied out with my apparently vain battle with Fortune, chance called me to another field of adventure.

There were in that year, all told, very certainly no more than seventy or seventy-five persons living in the Valley of Honey Lake. Of these, the larger proportion were engaged in ranching and stock-raising. Among them, the leading men were, after Governor Roop, Peter Lassen, W. T. C. Elliott, more familiarly known as Ruff Elliott, the Bass Boys, David Titherington, Tom Harvey, the Spencers, Captain W. Hill Naileigh, David Blanchard, Albert Smith, Orlando Streschley, Ed Mulrooney, Laninger, Storff, Watson, Kingsberry, Doc. Slater, and a few others.

At this time, the Washo and Pah-ute Indians were in the neighborhood. Occasionally, they appeared quite friendly, and would do a spell of work for the settlers, taking provisions in payment for such labor as they might choose to do.

No sooner, however, had they a good supply on hand than they would indulge in their natural propensity for stealing stock, frequently running off thirty or forty head of cattle at a time. It made no difference to them whether these were working oxen or milch cows, so long as they had horns. As none of the settlers were wealthy men, this unscrupulous appetite for marauding upon their stock was exceedingly disgusting. Treaty after treaty had been made with the Indians, and were equally worthless, whenever they had a fair show for stealing cattle with the chance of escaping retributive justice.

At length, the matter came to a head. The red robbers had run off nearly the whole of the stock belonging to a particular friend of mine. The nearest neighbors held an immediate meeting and determined, if possible, upon tracking the rascals and bringing them to book.

Arming ourselves, we started at once in pursuit. Striking their trail, which was very plain, we continued after them for the best part of two days.

In the noon of the second day, discovering that they were pursued, the Indians resorted to the cowardly expedient of killing the whole of the cattle. They cut open their sides, and let out their intestines, afterwards scaling the side of the mountain, to the north-east of the valley in which we had sighted them.

It was a lamentably pitiable spectacle to see the poor brutes moaning their moan of death, with their glazing eyes turned upon those who had come too late to save them.

Out of gun-shot, the Pah-utes—for the cruel scoundrels

belonged to this tribe—taunted us in no very heroic style. This was effected by extending their hands in front of their noses, as well as by a most expressive and insulting pantomimic slap on a very significant portion of their bodies. Blackguardism seems confined to no special race or country. So, at least, it appears to me.

After a brief council of war, pursuit was decided upon, and we began to mount the precipice. Harry Arnold was with me, and we managed to delude the Indians into the belief that they were beyond the range of our rifles, by letting the few shots we considered it advisable to fire, fall short of them. This ruse tempted one of them on an eminence at some distance, to repeat his aggravating gesture.

"I believe I can pick that scamp off with my old Kentucky rifle, Harry!"

"He's more than three hundred and fifty yards off, Mose!"

"I don't think he is."

"If any man can fetch him, you or I can. It's worth trying."

He had scarcely concluded when the crack of my rifle was heard.

The Pah-ute, who had been standing up in a more defiantly noble position than previously, uttered a loud yell, bounding into the air and rolling over the edge of the cliff, on to the rocks below.

His mashed and mangled body furnished me with his scalp. The shot, however, fair as it was, had been an ill-advised one. Its result was, that when we reached the bluff on which he had been standing, not another of the red scoundrels was visible. Nor did any of them show themselves after this, even at double the distance which had tempted him to indulge in such an insulting gesticulation.

On returning home, we found the whole of the valley, or, rather, those of its inhabitants who had not formed part of our party, in a state of intense excitement. The Indians had threatened a general massacre of the whites in it, if they refused immediately to leave it. It may be readily imagined, the death of the Pah-ute brave was ill-adapted to mollify such a determination. Under these circumstances, it was decided, should the affair come to the worst, on giving the red-skins as warm a reception as was in our power. But, in the meantime, Peter Lassen and one or two of the older settlers, with Governor Roop, were despatched to Pyramid Lake to hold a conference with Win-a-muc-ca, the Pah-ute chief, and, if they could do so, make a treaty with him.

This was effected. We had to give a certain number of head of cattle, several thousand pounds of flour, sugar, and tobacco, as well as many other small articles, in order to remain unmolested. It was neither more nor less than tribute.

It is said that years bring wisdom. In any case Age had decided against an Indian war in the neighborhood of Honey Lake Valley. Youth necessarily had to submit.

The demands of this treaty were a severe drain upon the settlement, the more especially as the winter set in early, with unusual severity. We were for more than four months shut in from the outer world, not even being able to reach Indian Valley, where we had been accustomed to have our wheat ground. It was ground during this time in a coffee-mill, and being out of coffee, we were compelled to use roasted barley as a substitute.

In addition to this, we had robbed ourselves of blankets to supply the Indians; and in this comparatively destitute condition, it was at times a difficult matter to supply the wants of the women and children.

Towards the close of the following year the Indians again became troublesome, until, in 1859, another treaty was patched up with them.

During this period one of the most popular and estimable men in the settlement, named Painter, was shot by a party of Pah-utes, who were in ambush at the head of Surprise Valley. Intelligence of this was brought us, by two or three companions who had been with him.

Painter's brother Ben applied to myself and some others to accompany him and bury the body. When we reached the spot, we found it cut and mutilated in the most frightful manner. Ben, with the rest of us, kneeling beside it, took a solemn oath to be avenged, whenever the opportunity was afforded us. Having then buried the body, we named the valley Painter's Cañon. It holds this name to the present day.

In the fall of the same year, a report spread that a man called Foreman had struck a valuable silver-mine in the vicinity of Black Rock. This was the same place, in which one of the settlers had discovered a large lump of silver ore. His name was Harding. Being on a hunting expedition at the time, and out of lead, he had run it into bullets.

A tolerable degree of excitement was caused amongst us, by the confirmation of previous suppositions, we presumed was thus given. But Black Rock was more than a hundred and twenty miles beyond Susanville, on the north-west side of Queen's River Desert. Its distance prevented many from going to prospect the place. However, after two or three days' talk over the matter, old Pete Lassen, with a man named Clapp, myself, and two other of the boys, determined upon verifying this report. On the following day, therefore, striking the old Emigrant Road, and continuing it as far as Granite Creek, our little party followed the Granite range of mountains up to Stove-pipe Springs. Thence, we crossed them to the Black Rock range. On the whole of the way, recently, we had encountered wandering Indians. They had seemed very friendly. We were, however, in a section of the country which the red-skins evidently considered their rightful property.

The place of encampment this night, selected by Uncle Peter, was very unfavorably situated. But when I advised him to allow me to select a more defensible location, on higher ground than that adjoining the small creek which he had chosen, the old German was obstinate.

"Tamn it, my poy! Don't you 'spose I know dem vellers. Dey von't hurt old Pete. You must give dem some crub, my poy! Dat ish all dey vants."

"That may be, Uncle Peter," I replied; "but I wouldn't trust the last three or four lots of red devils we have met, out of the range of my rifle."

Just at this moment a party of some dozen Indians approached the little camp, and the peaceful Peter motioning them with his hand, shouted out:

"Comes t'here!"

Understanding his inviting action, if not his words, they flocked around him. The old Dutchman gave them some bread, meat, and tobacco. Before they left us, he added to these things some powder and caps.

"A very dangerous gift," as I grumbled out in a low tone of voice.

When, after having got all they could, they quitted us, I expressed my wish to Uncle Pete to stand on guard during the night.

"Don't be a tamned vool!" was his reply. "I dink you ar' scared of dem Injins. If you vants, go on de hill, and leaff old Pete by himself. I hafe no vear."

Irritated by his answer, I blurted out:

"As you are determined to stay here, Uncle Peter, we'll not leave you."

But although, shortly after, the rest who were with him followed the old Dutchman's example, and after a smoke—the usual night-cap of the scout or trapper, spread out their blankets and prepared for rest, I was unable to do so. The unerring presentiment, which, without inspiring terror, tells us to be prepared for danger ahead, kept me on the watch. It was, therefore, at an early hour I aroused the camp.

"I'll pet," exclaimed the Dutchman, wrathful at what he considered his untimely wakening, turning to Clapp, " dat Mose vas not sleep all night."

"I tell you," was my sharp reply, "we had better get out of this place, cursed quickly!"

All of them, the old man excepted, turned out. In spite of Clapp's remonstrances, he, however, re-rolling himself in his blanket, petulantly exclaimed:

"Vell! I shleeps, some more."

It was scarcely a quarter of an hour after this, when we were fired upon from the craggy rocks which commanded our position. This volley slaughtered two of our doomed band. With very pardonable anger, although I have since regretted this ebullition of temper,

I administered a sharp kick to the form of Uncle Peter, who was rolling out of his blankets.

"Get up, at once," I sung out. "I suppose you'll follow my advice, now."

"Dey von't hurt old Pete," he responded, "so I vill get my plankets."

Thoroughly out of patience with him, I leaped into my saddle, and it was none too soon. Another volley took down Clapp, who was just mounting. Thinking, at last, there might be some danger, the Dutchman made a spring for Clapp's horse. In consequence of the saddle not being properly girthed, it slid round with him, and he fell to the ground. Before he could spring to his feet, the concealed Indians had put two bullets through his body. Then, quitting their hiding-place, they rushed upon me. One ball from my rifle settled the foremost of them. With a vigorous thrust from my heels to the flanks of the horse I was mounted on, I shook out my bridle and fled, in the midst of a perfect shower of bullets and arrows. All but one of the last missed me. This inflicted a scalp-wound, and for a moment I reeled in my saddle.

Turning immediately after, I once more raised my rifle, and had the satisfaction of wiping out one more Indian life, as a partial payment for the four they had taken.

Fairly out of danger of pursuit, I groaned over the death of Peter Lassen and my three companions.

No longer, my anger (the results had amply proved its justice) reproached him for the obstinate hardihood with which he had so untowardly ended our silver-hunting expedition.

Nevertheless, I was in no position to indulge either in

"The monument erected to Peter Lassen in Honey Lake Valley."
—*Page* 103.

wrath or sorrow. My present course was to be determined on. After a brief counsel with myself, I decided on continuing my flight through that part of the country settlers called the Desert. Few trees or rising hills marked this. Consequently I should here have less chance of risking a second Indian ambuscade. Indeed, on approaching Granite Creek, surrounding indications betrayed the presence of red-skins in the neighborhood, and although in want of water for myself and the animal I was mounted on, I preferred taking my chances on the comparatively barren plain.

Providentially, about nightfall I reached a spring. Here I dismounted, and gave my horse some two hours' rest.

Remounting, I then continued my way, piloting myself by the stars, as a fugitive on the Plains has frequently to do, if, as in the present case, although there was no moon, the night is clear enough to afford such a series of guide-posts to the wanderer.

Sunrise brought me to Smoke Creek. After another short rest, I again pulled out for Susanville.

The last fifty miles was hard work for the worn-out and jaded animal, whose enduring bottom had so largely contributed to my escape.

All in Susanville and around it were struck with horror, when I detailed the circumstances of the slaughter, from which I was the sole survivor. A large portion of the prominent settlers, amongst which Governor Roop was the most influential, coincided with me in denouncing all further treaties with the treacherous Indians, whether Pah-utes or of any other tribe.

However, some who had families, and were not unreasonably apprehensive for their safety in the event of a continuous struggle, warmly opposed our views. At this time, they believed that the red-skins around us numbered some eight or ten thousand.

In the face of their opposition, with the co-operation of Governor Roop, I determined upon a plan of action.

The first man I spoke to about joining me was Harry Arnold. He was a good shot, and a man of dauntless courage—not knowing what an impossibility might be. Not only did he consent to work with me, but gave me invaluable assistance in drawing together such tough and determined fellows as each of us could rely upon. Amongst these was Ben Painter, Luther Spencer, David Blanchard, my old friend Brighton Bill, Butch' Hasbrouck, and a number of others, as good men as ever rammed a ball down a rifle. In all, on the succeeding day, when we compared notes, we found twenty-four men had signed the roll, and pledged themselves to readiness at twenty minutes' notice. Both agreeing these were enough, we met on the following day in Willow Creek Valley, some fourteen to sixteen miles north of Susanville, where we completed our organization. The company was to take the name of the BUCKSKIN RANGERS, of which I was to be the captain. Harry Arnold and Ben Painter were chosen as my first and second lieutenants, while every one else was to act as an orderly sergeant, as well as his own commissary. Our agreement was that we should all dress in buckskin, at our own expense. Indeed, every man was to furnish his entire fit-out, complete for active service.

It will afterwards be seen, what this active service actually meant.

The next thing we had to do, was to select our horses.

Jack Bird, settled at the lower end of Honey Lake, owned a large stock. Besides presenting me with one of his own special favorites, to which he had given the name of the Tipton Slasher, he contributed to mounting the Rangers, most liberally.

The animal he gave me was a dapple iron-gray, partly of Spanish stock, with fine clean limbs, and of great speed and endurance. When Jack gave it to me, he said:

"Look here, Mose! if you ever let a darned red-skin catch you, it will be when you are not on Tip's back."

So much for the horse. Now, for myself.

Here was another change in my life. Circus-rider, pop-corn merchant, actor, detective, enlisted in an emigrant-train, gold-digger, and engaged with stock, I was now a ranger, and about to start in a new avocation. Hitherto, the red men I had come across had been looking after me and mine. Now, I was about to look after them.

The wild, dense forest, the gigantic mountains, the untrodden wilderness, sweeping beneath the sky with its varying swell, the unbroken waste and desert with the savage dwellers in it, whose crimson hands were against all civilization and gory with the uncounted murders of the white man, were now to furnish me with all the delight my nature could crave from a life of constant excitement. If I thought of my home and my friends, hundreds upon hundreds of miles away from me, I fear, at this time, it was with no inconsolable feelings of regret. In truth, I was about to become the veritable pioneer and protector of the scarcely-rooted civilization in which my lot had lately been cast. What chance was there I could over-much think of the past, in the absolute toil and the positive demand for vital activity of the present?

I was now about twenty-four years of age. My frame always promising strength, had become robust and powerful. Nature had gifted me with a sufficiently good constitution, as well as some considerable amount of energy. In addition to this, I possessed self-confidence enough to render me equal to the position in which fortune and adventure had placed me.

By the bye, it may be as well for me here to say a few words respecting Jack Bird, who was commonly called by his acquaintances "the" Captain.

About fifty-five years of age, and rather above the medium height, he possessed a powerful frame. Of dark complexion, and with piercing hazel eyes; he was a Mississipian, or, as he was used to say, he "came from old Massisip." In a word, a native, as he himself told me, of Arkansas, he was a splendid specimen of the class of men raised between civilized life and the extreme frontier of that civilization. Thus he had been made a backwoodsman by nature and predisposition, as well as necessity. With an active and energetic mind, he had carved out for himself in this wild country, a comparative fortune.

Had he been reared in New York State, he might have grown to the proportions of a Vanderbilt.

As, however, he had neither ferries to cross, nor railways to lay out, he occupied himself in traversing mountains, and in creating settlements. Not having legislatures to buy up, his restless energy had occupied itself in the control of savage life. An emigrant to California in 1849, he had engaged at first in mining. Afterwards, he went into stock-raising. It had been in 1857 that he settled on the boundaries of Honey Lake. Here he remained, until the close of the late war. Then, he decided upon returning for a brief period to his old homestead. He was, however, doomed never to reach it. Starting overland by stage, he was slaughtered, with the driver and other of the passengers, by the Indians, and never reached the place of his birth. He was one of the far too numerous victims, thrust forward by the restless progress of the day, in the face of the red savages, who have up to the present time been sheltered under the protecting ægis of our Government. A nobler, kinder-hearted, and franker man, perhaps, I have never met with.

It was somewhat previous to the formation of the Buckskin Rangers, to whose efficiency he had so largely and liberally contributed, that new silver-mines had been discovered, near what is now known as Virginia City, as well as in Gold Hill near Carson City, in Nevada. This discovery had created considerable excitement, and a large number of fortune-seekers were already flocking to the mines. The Indians, however, were quite as active as the searchers after wealth. Scarcely a day passed which was unmarked by the murder of some poor prospector, in that vicinity.

Their scalped remains invariably attested the means by which they had met their death.

The red-skins seemed almost as ubiquitous as devils. Wherever they passed, the trail of blood was left behind them.

In order to put a stop to their murderous depredations, Major Ormsby, at that period, well known throughout the country, in the neighborhood of Carson City, formed a company. Another smaller company, which had organized in Virginia City, for the same purpose, and already started out for the Pyramid Mountains, near the Reservation, had also joined him. Altogether, this party numbered something over one hundred and fifty men.

Large as this body was, it was destined to meet with ill-luck, or, probably, I should give it a much graver name.

Finding that the Indians had retreated into the mountains, Ormsby determined on advancing upon them, and driving them from their stronghold.

In doing so, he probably counted upon punishing them with a severity, which should free the neighborhood for some length of time from their murderous presence.

Whether it arose from his ignorance of the mode of warfare pursued by the red-skins, or from his over-confidence in his own numbers, it would be impossible now to determine. All I know is, that Ormsby's command was met with a terrific fire, which drove them back.

Whilst they were in full retreat, their enemies broke from their cover, and created a thorough panic in their ranks.

This resulted in a frightful disaster. Out of the hundred and fifty men, barely nineteen made their escape, the Major himself being among the slain.

The news of this terrific slaughter spread from settlement to settlement in the vicinity, like wildfire. But, previously, having heard of Major Ormsby's intended movement, the Rangers had decided upon lending him a helping hand. I had consequently moved with them from Honey Lake, upon the opposite side of Pyramid Mountains. On our way there, we had picked up a considerable number of volunteers, and counted some forty-five or fifty men in all. On reaching the base of the mountains, I found that it would be impossible to use our horses in any farther advance. We consequently decided upon leaving our four-footed companions, and I detailed half a dozen of our party to look after their safety.

After carefully examining our weapons, we then cautiously commenced ascending the rocky declivity.

Scarcely had we counted upon the almost immediate result of this step. Some three quarters of an hour after, we entered on a heavy mist or fog, which gradually became thicker and more dense, until it almost felt like a wet and sodden blanket, actually saturating us to the skin.

Suddenly, from the midst of this sheet of gloom, burst a spear of lightning. No! not a spear. It was, or seemed to be, one broad sheet of flame, which actually enveloped us, for the moment, blinding our eyes, and rendering us unable to see any of our companions.

This flash was followed by another and another, with incredible rapidity, until their scathing glow seemed almost continuous, while the roll of the unintermittent thunder made the mountain-side tremble beneath our feet.

By the first effect of this fearful storm, all our rifles had been instantly and involuntarily discharged. Stalwart men, who would have kept their feet in any ordinary commotion of the elements, were prostrated on the earth. Brave men, who had faced danger of almost every description, trembled like the veriest children. Their bronzed cheeks whitened with fear, and when able to stand, their knees quivered under them with terror. Perhaps none of us expected to escape from that shroud of living light alive. Very certainly I did not, and am not ashamed to own, that, in the midst of the rolling thunder, a cry to God for mercy, which none but the Almighty One Himself could possibly have heard, broke from my panting lips.

Possibly, that unpremeditated appeal was listened to. Soon after the flashes relaxed their continuity, and in its occasional pauses the thunder might have allowed the voice of any who had spoken to be heard. Gradually, the tempest passed away, and I heard a rough male voice say:

"The Lord be thanked!"

There was, in all probability, not one of us, un-church-going and reckless as we had all for many years been, who did not, within his own heart, re-echo that solitary thanksgiving.

CHAPTER VIII.

SCOUTING AND ITS RESULTS—CAUGHT NAPPING—FRANTIC WITH TERROR—"WHO HAVE BEEN TRIMMED SO NEATLY"—MY FAT FRIEND IN A PICKLE—PERSPIRATION AND BULLETS—THE REQUEST TO "SWAP" TREES—VIRTUE ITS OWN REWARD—HIGH TREASON TO UNCLE SAM—GOING OUT FOR GAME—AN UNPLEASANT MEETING—THE TUSSLE FOR LIFE—PUTTING AN END TO AN ORATION—"A TUFF 'UN."

ORDERS were shortly after given to continue the ascent, and in a sufficiently brief space of time, we had mounted above the belt of dark clouds, which were now drifting along the mountain-side beneath us, into a fresh and warm sunshine.

The revulsion in our feelings was almost instantaneous. Those who had quaked before, were now inclined to jeer at their own fright. Lips that had been whitened with terror were now actually laughing. Indeed, I much doubt whether he, whose involuntary audible piety had announced its feelings a few moments since, would have thanked any of us for reminding him of the exclamation. Very certainly, none of us did. We had, at any rate, the grace, not, in our present security, to scoff at the thanks in which we had so cordially although quietly participated.

When we were thoroughly above the heavily wet mass of cloud, we paused to rest and dry our clothing.

Then, having examined our weapons and reloaded them, we continued our progress in the direction in which it was supposed the Indians were to be found.

Night at last overtook us, and orders were given for camping. After a brief sleep of some four hours, with Harry Arnold, Butch' Hasbrouck, and Brighton Bill, I started out to find the position of the Indians. After we had moved in almost complete silence for a distance of some three miles, the faint light of their camp-fires might be seen by us. Touching Butch' and Bill, I in a whisper ordered both of them to remain where we then stood, and with Arnold crept quietly in the direction of the dying embers. Here, in their presumed security, were slumbering the men who had slain nearly the whole of Major Ormsby's party.

As yet, we were unaware of this fact, and I had only the knowledge of old Pete's death, and those of my other three companions, to square with the red rascals, whether they had any hand in that affair or not.

In consequence of this, I and Harry took a good survey of their situation, and, as noiselessly as we had approached it, returned to our own camp, taking Butch' and Brighton Bill with us, on our way. There we speedily aroused all the boys, and telling them we had spotted the game, bade them make ready. The night was clear and cold, although cloudy overhead, and in five minutes more we were upon our way, with an imperative injunction, upon my part, of perfect silence. This was perhaps needless, as few of the Rangers or those who had volunteered with us were novices in Indian fighting.

When I had, with Arnold, made my reconnoissance, we had thoroughly examined the position of the Indian camp. It was placed upon the summit of a precipice some two hundred and fifty feet in height, which beetled over a cleft or ravine in the mountain of considerable width.

On the side which we had approached it, it had been entirely unguarded.

Had it not been for their defeat of the large party under Major Ormsby on the preceding day, they would, even in such a position, scarcely have neglected to keep a watch.

However, now, from our side of the mountain, they had not any suspicion of the possibility of an attack.

But, although unable to count their positive number, Harry Arnold and myself had seen that they were exceedingly numerous; at the very least, six or seven times outnumbering our own party. It was, therefore, a matter of absolute necessity for us, even in taking them by surprise, to secure every possible advantage of position, in order to counterbalance this disproportion. To the left of the camp, in the rear of the plateau occupied by the slumbering red men, the ground rose more precipitously than it did on the side from which, some three hours earlier, we approached them. A portion of the boys, under the command of Arnold, was therefore detailed to this spot, while the remainder crouched under cover where it, at the time, was.

After this we waited impatiently for the rapidly coming dawn. This was a necessity, that we might have sufficient light to catch the sights of our rifles. We dared not throw away a single shot.

A long red streak, like a band of flame, colored the eastern horizon when the Indians began to stir. The first of the unconscious savages had risen to his feet, when my order rung out sharp and clear:

"Fire!"

The red-skin fell, and in an instant all was terror and confusion in the doomed camp.

Startled and confused by the sudden volley which was delivered with slaughterously fatal precision, the scarcely awakened red-skins leapt to their feet. Then came a volley from the party of Rangers with Harry Arnold. It was followed by another from mine. I had taken the precaution of ordering every other man to fire with each discharge, so as to give the preceding marksmen time to reload. Like clock-work rang out our deadly rifles, each shot dropping a man.

Fright had almost maddened the Indians, from the first intimation we had given them of our presence. Some ran from side to side of the plateau, looking vainly for a chance to escape. Others attempted to scale the declivity on which my portion of the boys were posted, and the rocks above which Harry held his position, in the very face of our fire. A few stood and endeavored to return us what we were giving them. However, they were considerably below either party; consequently, their shots rattled on the rocky sides of either slope short of us.

Again and again our untiring volleys rang out on the no longer quiet dawn.

Then, actually frantic with terror, many of the doomed savages leapt from the brink of the precipice. Others contrived to scramble over the broken edge of it, on the precarious and jutting portions of which they would scarcely, even in mid-day, under other circumstances, have trodden. In less than probably ten minutes from our first fire, not a living Indian remained in the camp where they had lately been sleeping. On examining this—for it would have been useless and, perhaps, dangerous for us to follow the runaways—we found enough to convince us that the white men had lately been severely punished. Scalps, shot-pouches, and carbines, with other tokens, were hurriedly left behind in their flight, to testify to this.

"We were not quick enough after the red devils, Mose!"

Arnold said this, as, with a positively qualmish sensation in my throat, I was standing upon that stony stretch of level ground which was now reekingly slippery with blood.

"We had better leave at once for the place where our horses are."

"I'd like to know who the whites were the darned scoundrels have trimmed so neatly?"

While saying this, he was meditatively turning over two scalps which lay on the gore-stained rock, beside a motionless red-skin, now as scalpless as the bodies from which he had taken them.

"P'raps," ejaculated Brighton Bill, whose feelings had in the last few years marvellously changed in regard to the legitimate manner of fighting the red-skins, "they be some o' Hornsby's chaps."

"Nonsense!" exclaimed Harry.

"Bill!" I said, "do you think the Major would have been such an idiot as to get trapped by the red skunks?"

"Why not? 'E mightn't be h'as thundering cute as you h'are, Cap!"

Unfortunately, as we soon discovered, my English friend was right in his supposition.

The sun had just risen when we started on our return, and before we reached the place where we had picketed our horses under guard the preceding day, we fell in with two of the survivors of the ill-fated party, and learned from them the details of the massacre, for which we had unwittingly just taken so large and wholesale a vengeance. This information completely obliterated every trace of compunction, for the morning's even more wholesale slaughter, which I had previously felt.

Crossing over to the south side of Honey Lake Valley, we followed it up to Captain Bird's old ranche.

After passing it, we found every house and farm empty and stripped of all that was in any way portable. The whole of the stock had also been driven off. But for the tramp of our hoofs, this portion of the valley would have been as silent as a desert.

"I'd say, Cap!" exclaimed Butch', "the cuss'd red devils had been here, too—only there are no dead men, laying round promisc'ous like."

Upon reaching Epstine's Ranche, we discovered the meaning of this. The owner, Joe, here informed us, the news of Ormsby's death, and that of most of the men with him, had reached the upper end of the valley on the day before. A complete terror had seized upon the whole of those then dwelling in it, and a general stampede had taken place amongst them for Dr. Slater's Ranche, above what is now the town of Janesville.

"Howev'r I guess'd I'd wait a bit, and see what turn'd up."

He was fingering his rifle, as he made the last observation. But on receiving the information of our retaliation his face brightened, and he gave utterance to a guttural exclamation of fierce and somewhat blasphemous delight, to which it will be needless for the pen to do justice.

On arriving at the ranche where he had told us his brother settlers had taken refuge, we found the men hard at work building a regular stockade around a cabin, which had the year previous been erected for the double purpose of a school-house and Masonic Hall. In spite of the joy with which our intelligence was received, they did not however desist from their labors. And, possibly, they were right, as the Indian troubles continued, and though the savages refrained from positively besieging the stockade while the Buckskin Rangers were around, they on one or two occasions ran off large quantities of the stock.

During the remainder of the season, we were occupied in a continuous scouting through this entire section of the country.

It was during one of our expeditions that Tom Harvey, one of us, was the subject of a good joke.

Human nature, in whatever situation it may be placed, has always a ludicrous side. Commonly, indeed, humor would almost appear to be the twin-sister of sorrow. They would, indeed, seem to walk through life, leaning upon each other, and hand in hand, to the very edge of the grave. The marvellous creations of Shakespeare's genius partake well-nigh equally of Tragedy and Comedy. Even so was it with the Buckskin Rangers, and their leader may be pardoned if he presumes to recall one of those creations (without the remotest hope of rivalling the intellect he has just called attention to) with the view of justifying himself.

"Falstaff" was most undeniably, as he has been drawn by the great dramatist, a fat man. Wherever fat can be found, the spirit of Fun almost invariably selects it as the subject or perpetrator of a joke. Now Tom was a man of enormous dimensions, if not in length, very certainly in width. Brighton Bill once said of him, that:

"Hif 'e was 'ammered hout, 'e would be long henough to reach the Nor' Pole, hand find Sir John Franklin."

If he had not been slenderer than Tom, I think his scalp, the moment after Bill had uttered this observation, might very possibly have been in the possession of Harvey.

However, this is a digression.

On one of our numerous scouts we had left our horses, guarded as usual, and were passing up a small valley, covered with a scattering growth of diminutive and remarkably lean trees, when some Indians, concealed in a small grove immediately in front of us, pulled trigger. Luckily their fire drew no blood. But, as in such cases, it is natural for him who is the subject of such an unexpected attention to jump behind anything which may be at hand, to shelter himself, we, each of us, made for the largest and nearest tree. None of them were sufficiently broad to make any of us a tolerably good cover.

In this situation, Tom also made for a tree.

Its exaggeratedly narrow trunk, merely concealed his head and the centre of his prodigious frame. Butch', who was nearest to him, could not help crying out.

"Look out, Fattee, or we shall only have the middle of yer left."

"Hold your darned tongue, you infernal fool!" roared out Harvey.

While saying this he had dodged to the one side of the tree, to escape an arrow which whistled by the other. With commendable judgment, he lost no time in leaping to the side he had left. This exertion of agility saved him from a bullet.

Butch' had drawn a bead on the head of the red-skin

"'I forgive you, old boy!' panted out Tom, as he leapt back once more."—*Page* 119.

who had fired the last, and with a yell of agony, he toppled over, struck by the Ranger's unerring ball.

"I forgive you, old boy," panted out Tom, as he leapt back once more.

This time he was scarcely quick enough, as another ball passed through the flying portion of his Buckskin upper garment.

"Why don't yer hide yer fat carcass," sung out Butch' in fierce wrath. There was no more time for jesting. "If yer don't, we shall have to bury yer."

"How can I?"

As the perspiring Harvey screeched out this amidst a general chorus of laughter, he took another wild leap, which was not one bit too soon.

All this had taken place in considerably less time than I have occupied in recounting it, or I fear all would have been up with the too fat Tom. The tree which I had been fortunate enough to secure was a fairly large pine. From behind it, I had the luck of picking off an incautious red-skin, and was already sighting another, when I heard our fat companion's voice. He had (how he dared to look round, I never knew) moaned or rather barked out, in a plaintive way:

"For God's sake, Mose! swap trees with me."

The irrepressible scream of laughter with which this pathetic appeal was received by me, caused my shot to be useless. It missed the Pah-ute I was aiming at.

Temporary inability on the part of our boys, from the painfully absurd position of Harvey, to maintain a continuous fire, now induced the red-skins to show themselves more boldly. They quickly found the mistake they had made in doing so. A general although scattering volley stretched a third of them upon the earth. They then evidently changed their opinion, and once more getting under cover, rapidly scattered.

We pursued them a short way, when we were overtaken by the remainder of our party, which we had left in charge of our animals.

Remounting them, we again started in pursuit. The red rascals had met, however, with too warm a reception to wait for any further attention at our hands. They had cleared out, and made good their escape across the mountains.

For many days the luckless Harvey did not hear the last of his offer " to swap trees" with me. At length, I, who had refrained from cutting any of the tolerably coarse witticisms which were uttered at his expense, was obliged to remonstrate warmly with Butch' and Brightton Bill.

"Yer are right, Cap!" exclaimed the former. "But I sware, it war too good a joke."

"Wouldn't it be better to split 'im down, and splice 'is two hends?"

As Bill said this they both burst into a peal of laughter, loud enough to be called Homeric, by any but a backwoodsman. They were, however, two good fellows, for they spoke to the other Rangers, and after this, fat Tom Harvey was left in peace. How he discovered the hand, I had, in easing him off, it would be impossible to say, as I never knew. But some two days afterwards he came up to me and Harry Arnold, as we were riding along slightly in advance, and said:

"Mose! you're a darned good fellow, and I'll be blamed if I ever forget it."

"What do you mean, Tom?"

"For stopping the chin-music of them fellows. What on airth else, should I mean?

At the same time, he jerked his thumb across his shoulder in the direction of the rest of the party, who were at some little distance in our rear, very significantly.

"You see, Cap!" exclaimed Harry with a slight chuckle, "what the copy-book tells us, is right, after all."

"What are you driving at?"

"It says, Virtue is its own reward."

We had retraced our steps, passing Eagle Lake into Willow Creek Valley, on the far side of the range of hills which divide it from Honey Lake, until we arrived at the stockade built by the settlers, which has earlier been alluded to.

A few days subsequently, we struck into Long Valley, and having crossed Pea-vine Mountains, reached the Truckee River. Here we encamped, and on the next morning, following it for some distance, struck across the hills, towards the Sink of the Carson River. Passing this stream below Fort Churchill, we continued in a southerly direction until we came to the Walker River. Near it, we had a little brush with the Walker Indians, which did not detain us very long. During this, one of our boys received a slight flesh wound from an arrow. Why these red-skins have received this name is matter of question, as they are certainly a branch of the Pah-ute tribe. However, it had been given the savages in this small portion of the country, and while I was living in that section, of which it forms part, it stuck to them.

On the west fork of Walker River, we were met by a company of United States cavalry.

The officer in command inquired for our leader, and I presented myself.

He behaved very courteously in manner, although his orders, given to me with a degree of imperative sharpness, which was scarcely as courteous in reality, were by no means agreeable. His instructions were to make peace with the Indians, and he commanded us to return homewards. If we would not desist from our present employment, he told us, he should be obliged to arrest us and take us down to Fort Churchill. These peremptory orders were unpalatable to the last degree. But what could be done. He was Uncle Sam's servant in blue-coat, brass buttons, and shoulder-straps. We were children of the aforesaid Uncle Sam.

Like obedient boys, although most unwillingly, we concluded, after a brief hesitation, to bend our steps homewards.

With a cordial grasp of the hand—for, on finding we had so frankly accepted the compulsory situation, the officer unbent himself considerably—I bade him "Farewell," and we silently, for some time, rode along the course of the stream. The first words I heard subsequently, were some ten minutes after this. They came from the lips of Brighton Bill.

"Huncle Sam his nothing but a blasted hidiot."

Possibly, I might have been valuing some of his servants at much the same weight, but I was too good an American to stand such an expression of opinion from a Britisher. Turning in my saddle, I roared out:

"None of that. It's high treason. I'll be hanged if I haven't half a mind to ride after the blue-coats, and hand you over to them."

When I said this, there was a general laugh, and the

whole of us recovered, in some measure, our good humor.

After continuing about twenty miles along the road the soldiers had just traversed, we encamped about two o'clock in the afternoon, turning our horses out to graze, as there was good pasture in the neighborhood. Portion of the boys commenced cooking. Butch', having a somewhat more dainty tooth in his head on this occasion than usual, felt it crave for fresh meat, and said to me:

" 'Spose I go out, and kill yer something to eat."

" All right," was my answer. " You may find a Jack or two," meaning a Jack rabbit, " down the valley. I'll go up the cañon, and see whether I can't find some grouse."

Saying this, I had pointed to a small cañon on one side, stretching irregularly from the vicinity of our camping ground. At the same instant, Brighton Bill, who had been stretched on the cool turf with his eyes closed, leapt to his feet.

" You're hawful smart, hain't you, Mose ? Hi'll 'ave some hof that fun myself. If hi don't, blow me."

He, however, thought fit to try another cañon to the left.

For the first time since I had been an inhabitant of the Plains, I neglected to arm myself, as I had constantly been accustomed to, when scouting. The good servants of Uncle Sam, whom we had met earlier in the day, had travelled up the road. Of course they had sharp eyes. Besides, if the red-skins had seen them, they would certainly have got out of their way as quickly as possible. How should they know our Uncle wanted to be theirs, too ? Peace would be the very last thing they thought of, when they set eyes upon his uniform. So, thinking there could be no danger, I placed my sheath-knife in my belt, and taking my Kentucky rifle with me, started.

Walking carelessly up the cañon, now examining the trees for game, then scaling the declivity to the right, or pushing through the chapparal and the heavy timber, I had wandered on, for more than an hour.

Suddenly, in one of the thick and tangled clumps of chapparal, I fancied I heard the familiar note of one of the birds I was in search of. At once, I stopped to listen.

While standing there silent and motionless, it could scarcely have been more than fifty seconds, I heard a noise almost immediately behind. Instinct or experience, one or both, told me what that sound was. The red-skins had not been so scared by the advance of Uncle Sam's servants, as necessarily to refrain from a dash for one of his children, if the chance was given them. I felt the chance was now.

Turning immediately, I had barely time to see two Indians.

In another instant, before I could lift my gun to my shoulder, one of them had bounded towards me and wrenched it from my grasp, while the other sprung at me with the evident intention of clinching me. If I had then the time to think, I fear, loyal American as I might be, my thoughts might have corroborated Brighton Bill's opinions touching the sanity of Uncle Sam. Fortunately, I had no time to become critically disloyal. My hunting-knife had been drawn, and at the very moment when his hot and vindictively fierce breath came searingly to my face, was buried to the very hilt in his heart.

"He opened his mouth to gasp for breath; I was above him, and grasping a handful of sand, I forced it into his gaping mouth."—
Page 125.

As he fell, the other of my assailants, with my own rifle clubbed, struck me a heavy blow upon the shoulder. It nearly felled me to the earth.

Then, dropping the weapon, he sprang upon me, making a desperate clutch for the hand in which my knife was grasped. As he seized my wrist, I threw the knife from me as far as I could, and grappled with him. He attempted to draw his own. I, however, had grasped him by a peculiarly tender portion of his person, which modesty prevents me from naming. The pain of this prevented his using his knife, and in the contest we both fell on the sloping side of the cañon, clinched together firmly.

Now, commenced the struggle for life.

Rolling over and over, now on the short turf, and again amidst the dense and tangled chapparal—at one moment the red-skin would be above me, and in the next I would be stretched on his writhing body. Whenever I got the chance, and one of my hands free, I would seize a handful of sand, if it was within reach, and thrust it in the mouth and eyes of the Indian.

He was not slow in taking the lesson I gave him. He began to follow suit.

After rolling down the side of the cañon for some hundred yards or more, panting with the desperate struggle, he opened his mouth to gasp for breath. At the time I was above him, and grasping a handful of sand, I forced it into his gaping mouth.

It had its effect. Literally choking with the enforced dose, he loosened me. At the same time, he violently threw up his hands, as a man might do in the agony of strangulation.

Then, with a supreme effort, I groped for his knife.

Having found it, I drew it from its sheath, and, at last, the terrible struggle which had been forced upon me was over.

When, at occasional times, I recall it now, it seems to my recollection as if that brief contest for existence had nearly maddened me. Scarcely did I appear to possess consciousness of any of my actions. And yet, I know that I inflicted on him some fifteen to twenty wounds, any one of which might or must have been a fatal one.

As I found myself once more upon my feet, it was a tolerably difficult matter for me to realize that I was still living.

While engaged in attempting to do so, the whole landscape seemed to quiver vaguely under my fading eyes. Its lines and colors fairly danced before me. I felt that I was falling, and everything around settled into a dense blackness.

I knew no more.

On, after some time, recovering my senses, I found that I was lying by the side of the Indian, literally drenched with the blood flowing from his wounds. Sitting up, after a few minutes, I was enabled to recall my lagging senses and realize the struggle I had gone through. Yes! there it lay, stark and motionless in the shadow thrown across it from the rocky side of the cañon, by the sun which was now far beneath it. As for the corpse beside me, it was stabbed and hacked in a frightful manner. But for the fearful strife I had been engaged in with it, when living, and the danger I had, as it seemed to me, so unaccountably escaped, I should positively have sickened at the sight. The memory of this strung my nerves once more to endurance, although my garments were dripping with its blood, and absolutely soaked through with my own sweat.

Staggering to my feet, I re-collected my senses, which had, for a short space, again wandered. Then, with some difficulty, I again ascended the rough hill, until I reached the space on which the first Indian, I had made an end of, was lying. His teeth were forced together—his eyes staring unconsciously up to the blue sky. My knife was at some distance from the spot. The rifle was close to him. Its barrel was bent and its stock broken with the heavy blow I had received.

Let me squarely own that never, either before or since, have I raised the hair of any Indian, with a more secure feeling of angry joy than I felt in taking those two scalps.

I had now to return.

The position of the sun, low beneath the western summit of the cañon, testified to the fact that some two hours must have elapsed since the two Pah-utes had leapt upon me.

Slowly, and with great difficulty, I commenced my way towards the camp. While looking on the scene of my danger, I had been kept up by the remains of the excitement I had experienced. I had felt no pain, and been unconscious of fatigue. Now, my dead enemies lay unconsciously on the earth. The exhaustion consequent on my fierce struggle for life, and the suffering from the blow upon my shoulder, became apparent to me. Scarcely, was I able to walk. Frequently was I obliged to lean on a jutting boulder of rock, or steady myself for a minute or two against the trunk of a tree, before I could again persistently renew my progress. Not yet had I reached the mouth of the cañon, when some of the boys met me.

It seemed that Butch' and Brighton Bill had long since returned, and, although scarcely alarmed, had grown in some slight degree uneasy at my not putting in an appearance. Consequently, with some of the others, they had come out to seek for me.

No sooner was I seen by them, than they shouted out to me. My lips strove to frame a shout in reply. But even to myself, my voice sounded a long way off. It was so faint and low that they did not hear a word.

Rushing towards me, Bill cried out:

"What his the matter, Mose?"

Butch' demanded:

"Have yer got any game?"

The only answer I could give them was to hold out the two scalps I had taken.

Startled by this and my struggling silence, for they knew I was attempting to speak, they looked at my dress, and in spite of the fading light, saw its torn and dilapidated condition, and the blood with which it was smeared and streaked almost in every part. Bill gave a groan, and said:

"Get Mose to the camp, Butch'! Hi'll go hand look hafter 'is rifle, before some hother thieving Hingin cusses find hit."

In an another instant Ben Painter had lifted me, and throwing me, gently enough, although it caused me frightful suffering in my shoulder, across his own, strode down the cañon. Indeed, so great was the pain from the merciless blow I had received, that I remember little beside it, until I found myself sitting on the ground, leaning against Painter's knee. The whole of the upper portion of my dress had been stripped off, while Butch' was bathing the black and swollen flesh which had been struck with the clubbed rifle. How it happened that no bones were broken by it, is, even now, a marvel to me.

When they found me again able to speak, the boys began to ply me with questions. But while I was answering them, Brighton Bill appeared on the scene.

His search of the ground on which I had run such a risk of being completely chawed up, must have been a pretty thorough one. He brought in, not only two rifles, but two United States blankets, several unopened boxes of caps, two cans of powder, and, in addition to these, a small keg of Uncle Sam's whiskey. This had already been opened, and may possibly account for the red rascals having forgotten the reason for which they had so liberally partaken of his bounty.

The whiskey was a veritable God-send, for we were out of the article. A tincupful (this time I did not ask for a second before eating) did more to put me to rights, and enable me to forget my pain, than the care which the Rangers had been bestowing on me.

"If ever there was a good Samaritan, Bill, you are one."

Let me here record the fact that Bill knew nothing about Samaritans, for good or evil. Nor, indeed, am I inclined to think, had any of the others a very correct idea of my meaning. Even the teaching of a New England Sunday-school had been forgotten, as I deeply regret being obliged to say one of the boys hailed from the classically Methodist locality of New Bedford.

But, if Brighton Bill was not well versed in Scripture, he displayed himself this evening in a new light—that of an orator. No sooner had he served round the whiskey which he had captured from the already slaughtered enemy, than he produced from one of the blankets in which he had wrapped it, my twisted and broken rifle.

"Jist look 'ere, boys," he said, "hat the popper of hour Cap. This h'is the harticle with which 'e smashed ha couple of Hingins. Hi'm blowed h'if you didn't, Mose! H'it's no huse 'iding your light hunder a bushel, when H'i 'ave the hevidence in my hown 'and, and show hit." Here I endeavored to put in a word, but it was drowned in the general applause, and seizing on the instant of its cessation, he continued: "H'if you 'ad only seen those blarsted Hingins. Wun of 'em stood seven an a 'alf foot 'igh in 'is stocking-feet, and the h'other—"

I could no longer refrain, but cried out:

"It's quite clear who tapped the whiskey keg, before we had a chance of looking at it."

The Britisher gazed in pathetic wonder on his partially maimed leader, as he heard this ungenerous insinuation against his sobriety. Then with a sadly melancholy smile, he said:

"H'i forgive you, Cap! But, may H'i be blamed if you harn't a tuff 'un."

That night, guard being kept by Butch' and Ben Painter, I slept well and soundly. On the next morning I was up by daylight, and we returned to Honey Lake through Carson City.

When we arrived there it was to hear that another treaty had actually been made with the Indians. Once more they were to be allowed to re-enter the valley. The settlers were to resume possession of their ranches, and what stock was left on them, or could be found. How long it would continue, the Devil and the red men themselves, only, could form an opinion.

CHAPTER IX.

The Pick, Pan, and Shovel—Somewhat Down in the Mouth—
"Roping in a Greeney"—The Shrewd Yankee—A Square
Meal, and a Bad One—No Gold—Nearly at Starvation
Point—The Elk, and how long it lasted—Mountain Meat
—Captured by the Indians—My Experience of the Stake
—Converted into a Candlestick—The Crack of a Dozen
Rifles.

In something less than two weeks, my shoulder was completely well, and the enforced inactivity had made me restless.

At this time, the vast treasures of gold said to be awaiting the miner in British Columbia, near Frazer's River, created great excitement through the West. The fever of this excitement was like all such fevers—contagious among the idle. Having then nothing to do, I caught it. In an informal meeting with several of the Rangers, I proposed to them that we should visit the new land of promise. As they were willing to accompany me, a full meeting was summoned. At this it was unanimously determined that the journey should be undertaken, if we could make it by land.

After some few days spent in the necessary inquiries, it was finally decided we should start for the recently discovered locality, where fortunes were believed to be awaiting the pick, pan, and shovel—as speedily as we could make due preparation for doing so.

This did not take any very great length of time. In less than a week the whole of us were in readiness.

And after a kindly, and, in some cases, more than kindly, farewell to our friends in Susanville and round Honey Lake, we put ourselves on the road to the new locality.

The natural rush and active whirl of my life during the last few years, had, by this, almost deadened my memory for those friends I had left in the East. He, who is from day to day almost carrying his life in his hand, has not overmuch time or wish for reflection. Occasionally, I would think of my wife and my other relatives. But I had not yet made enough, really to contemplate returning to them. Young still, it appeared to me that there were yet days and years sufficient before me, to dismiss all such dreams for, at any rate, the present.

In fact, as I have earlier said, I relished the constant change and dash of the life I had entered on.

It was no use disguising it, my nature was, in every respect, a vagrantly instinctive one, full of vaguely wild hope, it is true, yet mingled with an almost profound indifference to what the future chance might be.

Nevertheless, on the night before we had determined upon commencing our arduous journey, I could not help feeling somewhat down in the mouth. It was with a rare and scant attack of homesickness, which, however, passed away from me on the next morning, almost as soon as I found myself in the saddle.

It would be unnecessary for me to catalogue the various points we touched, through our course, in the fashion of a guide-book. This, the more especially as nothing of great interest occurred on the way, until, in due time, we struck Frazer's River, near Fort Hope.

Here we remained for a few days, in order to give

our animals the rest they needed. They had done us good service.

In this place, we found that the hunger for gold was drawing men of the same nature as ourselves, to the last-discovered Eldorado, from every part of the country. Young men who wished to grow wealthy without patient toil, and men more advanced in years, whose days of labor had as yet profited them little, with an occasional "rough" from one of the larger cities, whose reputation forced him into a new country, or the gambler, whose practice in "stocking the cards" or "roping in a greeney," had become too well known. Some few came also, whose talents should have enabled them to do battle with the world successfully, in any location they had chosen. Their reasons for seeking Frazer's River were, however, kept to themselves. None of my companions had sufficient time on his hands, or enough curiosity, to seek to draw the veil from the past life of any of them.

There were, however, some few who had tried the mines and were returning. Want of patience or want of luck, one, or, it may be possible, both of these had conjointly made them unsuccessful.

With neither gold in their pockets nor grub in their packs, these men were for the most part dead-broke, and heaped their imprecations on the country they were quitting in vigorously round terms. Nor could it be said, that granting their ill-fortune might somewhat have colored their opinions, these were too flattering.

One of these whom we met with, was a stalwart specimen of the shrewd Yank. I and Ben Painter had encountered him, wandering round in a disconsolately drifting manner, and with a hungrily wolfish look on his lean jaws, which inspired us with a degree of sympathy. Moreover, we were mentally "prospecting" the yet unseen diggings. The information he could give us, might be valuable. So, although provisions were already scarce, and even coffee a luxury, we asked him into the camp to share our evening meal, which, to tell the truth, was by no means too plentiful. After feeding, he honored us by saying:

"'Tarnation bad as yer supper is, it is the first square meal I've eat, for three days."

"How war that?" Butch' asked.

"Yer see, in the mines there war nothing to get for love or money. And here, I guess, there's darned little love unless yer can buy it."

"We heard that, up here, you had only to turn a shovel to find gold."

"And b'lieved it, as I did," he quietly growled out.

"Yer don't mean to say there are none," ejaculated Ben.

"I guess yer won't do more than any o' the rest on us."

"But, some must have had a fair share of success," I said.

"Why d' yer think so, Captain?" he drawled out, nasally.

"From the row about the diggings that has been made through the whole of the West."

"Well, I'll tell yer. I was one of the first that come out here, from Kalifornee. I'd been duing a smartish bit of business down thar. But I tell yer, the dollars didn't come in fast enough. Than, I heerd of this darned place, and thought I'd strike for it and find 'ile, sure. So, I made up a good kit o' things to last me two months, and sit out. Darn the diggings. I've been at work thar, more nor three months, and here I am at the first square meal I've sot down tu for three days, as I told yer before, and a darned bad one, too, as I said when I finished it."

"Then you don't believe there is much gold in this part of the country?"

"Thar may be, Captain!"

"What do yer mean, then?" inquired Ben Painter.

"I found none," drawled out the Yank as he slowly rose, "and by the 'Tarnal! I nev'r met one as has."

The groan that issued from the bottom of Brighton Bill's stomach, would, at any other time than this, have provoked mirth. It did not, however, do so now. The matter was far too serious for laughter.

If the disgusted Yankee had told us the truth, it was evidently no use for us to help thicken the crowd of deluded seekers for gold, thronging to the diggings. Provisions, as I have earlier said, were scarce. They were consequently dear. Our own stock had for several days been running low. What was to be done?

More inquiries were made by us. The replies, although varying in degree, were all of them confirmatory, more or less, of the Yankee's opinion.

After a brief council of war, the Rangers, therefore, decided upon striking once more for Puget Sound, in search of game. If we found it, we would kill enough for us to take our return-trail. Game, however, was scarcer in that locality than we had found gold to be in the neighborhood of Frazer's River. We had to betake ourselves to digging; not in the soil for the precious metal, but in the sand on the shore of the Sound for clams and mussels. Even these were rarely found by us. In short, the Rangers and their leader were reduced to the very verge of starvation. Nor did we run any risk of meeting any charitable person who might have the means of giving us ".one square meal," even if it were "a darned bad one."

In this strait, it was resolved on to start for the mountains, and take the chance of killing or being killed, to save us from dying by hunger.

Here, for the first two days, we met with scarcely anything. About noon on the third, I and Arnold were standing together. During the whole morning we had found no game, and were gazing around us with that sense of discomfort a continuously empty stomach is certain to produce in humanity, when we heard a shot in the distance. It was to the right of us. Almost immediately it was followed by another. As the two puffs of smoke drifted above the stunted pines which covered the unequally rough ground in that direction, I heard a sound which, faintly as it came to us, I immediately recognized, from the use of it by Brighton Bill. It was what he called:

"A 'onest British cheer."

"You know the voice, Mose?"

"Yes! Let's break for it."

We accordingly "broke" in its direction. Three more of the boys had already joined him and Ben Painter by the time we had arrived there. The two first mentioned had met with the good fortune of spotting a huge elk. The animal had been killed, and while still warm, the men were engaged in skinning him.

A fire was quickly kindled, and, by the time, portion of the elk was ready for our ravenous appetites, the remainder of the Rangers entered their names as partners in the welcome feast. For, that it was right welcome, my present remembrance of it unmistakably assures me.

Stopping here until we had jerked most of the meat on the elk's large carcass, we again started on our journey back.

Having travelled in an easterly course through a magnificently wooded country, we reached the Columbia River, near Fort Okimakane, and passing down it through the territory occupied by the Flat-head tribe of Indians, arrived at the Walla-Walla. Thence we crossed the Blue Mountains; and, after several days' more travelling through the rocky wilderness and broken cañons, arrived at the Owyhee, which, some distance higher up, we crossed and continued over the range of hills by the side of this stream, until we at length reached Surprise Valley.

We camped in this spot for two weeks, for the purpose of recruiting our horses and hunting up game. The jerked elk-flesh was already very nearly brought to an end.

It was, while we were in this neighborhood, that I met with an adventure which very nearly ended this volume before I had even written a page of it, if I may be pardoned the Irishism of this expression. But, for the opportune arrival of the Buckskin Rangers, my life would very certainly not have been worth an empty powder-can.

Early one sharply fresh morning, I had left the camp in the direction of High Rock Cañon. This was at a distance of some ten miles.

While upon my way, perhaps some six miles or more, I saw a mountain-sheep. Having a liking for wild mutton, I cautiously crept round the cliff upon which he was standing, to get a fair shot at him. At length reaching a spot from which I might consider myself fairly sure of the meat, I fired.

The shot told, and the animal fell.

However, instead of dropping where he stood, and where I could not inconveniently have become possessor of the toothsome flesh, the perverse sheep preferred rolling down the cliff.

Well! It would be some more trouble, but I could easily get him. I therefore went round to the base of the cliff. On arriving there, I could not help swearing a most ungodly oath. That wretched lump of mountain-meat had chosen to remain some half-way from the bottom on which I was, and the top of the precipice, on which he had been standing.

My readers may already have been enabled to give me credit for what I consider my resolution, although some of my good friends have not unoccasionally denominated it obstinacy.

It came very decidedly into play, upon this occasion.

I was determined not to be balked in my love for mountain-mutton. In accordance with my resolve, I prepared to climb after it. The face of the cliff was so steep and rugged that, in order to have the use of both my hands, I was compelled to relinquish my rifle. Therefore, depositing it where I stood, I commenced the ascent. Being a good climber, I naturally thought I should have no more difficulty than that which generally attends such an operation. Neither, had I. After reaching the jutting point upon which my mutton had so pertinaciously lodged, I dislodged it, and sent it down the rough precipice. It was now time to think of myself regaining the base of the cliff, in a less rapid mode. But, to descend was no child's play. Now I could not find the footing which I remembered previously having. Consequently, I was obliged to wriggle my body to one side or the other, in order to find a place to rest on. Afterwards, the rock would crumble under me, or fragments upon which my feet were resting would slip out of their bedding. Moreover, my sight was utterly useless. I had to depend upon the trained sense of feeling in my moccasined toes. Having covered some space of the face of the cliff, I began to find I was not descending it in the same direction in which I had ascended it. The cliff was sloping inwards. Again I had to climb and try a new line. This was apparently somewhat better. However, placing my feet upon the roots of a sage-bush, I was incautious enough to trust my whole weight to it.

It tore out from the face of the cliff.

When I felt it giving way, I threw out my hands to grasp at some support.

While falling, all the errors and faults I had committed, seemed to rush across my mind. Why it was, I know not, but the star-like eyes of Clo-ke-ta blazed upon my memory.

Then I struck the rocky ground beneath me, and, for the time, remembered no more.

Upon coming to my senses, I found that my hands were bound behind me.

Looking with scarcely conscious anger around, I saw several red-skins.

These, I presume, had been watching me, amusing themselves with my desperate efforts to descend the cliff, and calculating upon trapping me when I reached its foot.

No sooner had I seen them than the positive danger restored my senses.

Resistance was, however, useless. Raising me to my feet, they commenced driving me down the valley. Deliberately, I say, "driving." Nor was this driving done by any means in a merciful fashion. It was effected with heavy blows and sharp sticks, which were aimed at and thrust into my ribs and sides, with no pity.

For the moment, however, I was unconscious of this.

The red devils were going straight in the direction of our camp. Great God! If they only did not pause until they arrived there.

This was a futile hope.

They paused about two miles and a half from the place where my boys were. With a vain effort at being heard, I gave vent to a loud shout. A burly Indian struck me heavily across the mouth to silence what he haply considered my bravado. "I was a white brave, and I knew that I must die." It was natural red-skin reasoning.

Then spitting in my face, he spoke briefly in their guttural tongue, and in a few moments more I had been stripped of all my clothing, and compelled to stand with my feet about twenty inches apart. Stakes were driven into the earth by the side of these, to which my legs were tightly lashed. Then, planting in the ground other stakes at a short distance, my arms were extended at full length, and bound to them. A cord around my neck was fastened to another stake in my rear. In addition to this, two sharpened stakes were planted directly under my arm-pits. It was thus rendered almost impossible for me, even to stir.

No sooner had this been effected, than the entertain-

"The braves would squat upon the earth and rest, while their squaws subjected me to more horrible tortures than the mind could conceive without personal experience."—*Page* 141.

ment, for such they evidently considered it, commenced.

The *Mahalas* or squaws had been pointing splinters of grease-wood, about three inches in length. As the braves danced round me, whooping, yelling, or singing one of their wild war-songs, the squaws would strike the pointed splinters into my flesh and leave them sticking in it. After somewhat wearying of their share in this cheerful pandemonium, the braves would squat upon the earth and rest, while their squaws subjected me to more horrible torture than the mind of the white could conceive without personal experience. Human excrement was thrust in my face, and rubbed over my mouth. When they would pause awhile, it seemed as if they were only trying to invent some more disgusting and possibly more painful mode of torture.

But what is the use of prolonging such a recital?

This infernal orgy was kept up until night set in, when the climax of their devilish fury was capped by their taking burning brands from the fires which had been kindled, and igniting the splinters of grease-wood which they had thrust in my body.

It is absolutely impossible by mere words to convey any idea of even the tenth part of the agony which this caused me. Ten thousand needles, red-hot, seemed to be piercing my flesh and stabbing me in every part of my body with their lancing flame.

Up to this moment, I had not abandoned all hope.

Perhaps, the boys might come up in time to save me.

In my now maddening suffering, I actually prayed that it might end. Heaping every species of opprobrium on the red demons, that I could, in my own tongue, I added to them such galling Indian terms as I had been able to pick up during my life in the West. These were not over-numerous, but they would have been more than sufficient to have inspired the incarnate devils with a greater fury, and, in a few moments more, I should have been quit of all the trouble and suffering of the world in which I had been a dweller.

As this desire was surging incontrollably above my bodily agony, I heard the crack of a dozen rifles.

The same number of the Indians dropped in the very places on which they had been sitting or standing, and I knew that I was saved.

CHAPTER X.

BETWEEN TORTURE AND SAFETY—THE VALUE OF POPULARITY—
UNCLE SAM'S BLUE-COATS—A TRAPPING EXPEDITION—IN FOR
IT—THE CAPTURE OF MY FIRST PET GRIZZLY—SKINNING AND
CARVING—" PROSPECTING " FOR SILVER—A LIVING BLANKET—
DARKNESS AND THE SURPRISE—CARRIED OFF AS A CAPTIVE—
OUT OF THE THONGS—THE BUTT AND THE MUZZLE—WHO IS
THE REAL HERO ?

It seemed, that when I had not returned to the camp by dusk, the boys had begun to be somewhat uneasy on account of my prolonged absence. Butch' Hasbrouck then volunteered to hunt me up. Ben Painter was the only one with him. Although uneasy, none of them really believed I was in a serious difficulty. If they had, as Butch' subsequently said, when, some weeks later, talking the matter over with me, they would have had me " out of the tight place I war in, a good hour sooner."

It was not long ere they heard the noise made by the howling and yelling devils.

" There war something up," as Painter whispered to Butch'.

Then they crept nearer.

On discovering the light of the camp-fires, and recognizing through the trees the forms of the red-skins moving rapidly amongst them, they instantaneously concluded that I had been killed, and that the savages were celebrating the event in their own fashion. " By sheer luck," as Painter expressed it, they did not come near enough the *Campoody* or Indian camp to discover me.

Had they done so, they were two men only, and could not have saved me, although they might, or rather would, beyond any doubt, have made my death a somewhat costly one to the Indians, who would most certainly have finished me before their two rifles could have settled enough of the scoundrels to prevent their doing so.

They returned to the camp and told Arnold and the rest what they had seen.

If I had previously any doubt of my popularity with the boys, the result of the information thus given would have dispelled it.

In an instant every man was on his legs, and in another half-minute, armed with their rifles and revolvers, they were following the two scouts who had located the red-skins.

On drawing sufficiently near, they had discovered me.

It would be needless to recapitulate what I have already stated. Their plan was determined upon, and they carried it fully out. Not a single red-skin, male or female, nor even a *papoose*, was suffered to escape. Indeed, I believe that if any of Uncle Sam's Agents or Blue Coats had ventured to interfere with their prompt judgment, supposing they had been on the ground, it might have gone badly enough with them, in spite of our presumable loyalty.

All that night, I lay on my blankets, in terrible agony. It seemed as if I was losing my reason. A tough constitution and the care of my companions, however, brought me through my suffering. Let none tell me that men, rough as they may be, are unfitted to attend the sick. Brighton Bill and Butch' constituted themselves not only my medical men, but my nurses. They never left me for an instant. While one ate or slept, the other was at my side. Their rough hands were as gentle with me, as those of any woman might have been.

Arnold and Painter were also unceasing in their attendance.

Yet I feel that I am perhaps wrong in particularizing any of the Rangers, when all were so kind. Suffice it, therefore, to say, that after some ten days I was able to stand once more and move slowly about. The effects of my fall, and the Indian treatment after it, were obviated by the more civilized care and love, for I may surely call it so, the boys bestowed upon me. In something less than a fortnight I was able again to ride, and we started for Honey Lake Valley.

On reaching it, winter was just approaching, and as peace had been promised by the chief of the Pah-utes, I foresaw there would be little occupation for me during this season. So, after a little talk, Butch' Hasbrouck and Brighton Bill agreed to go with me, on a trapping expedition to the Humboldt River. Providing ourselves with the necessary number of traps and other requisites, we in a few days started, pitching our camp in the Lassen Meadows, at La Due Very's, generally known as "Old Bible-back," on the banks of that stream. For some time we were very successful; indeed, as we afterwards found, remarkably so, gathering together a large number of beaver, otter, and other skins. Then, needing a re-supply of many necessary articles, we struck back to the valley, and finished the winter near the Black Buttes. Here we had as great a success in trapping mink, marten, and foxes.

It was while we were here, that I had the satisfaction of killing my first grizzly.

Early on one sharply cold morning I had started out

7

to make the round of our traps. As I entered a dense chapparal, I saw, moving towards me, a large bear with two young cubs. Of course it was their dam, and I knew I was in for it. If I had taken to my heels, I felt assured the speed of the ungainly brute would exceed mine. There was no large tree near, in which I might have taken refuge. She had already seen me, and her small, twinkling eyes were sparkling like black diamonds. Naturally, therefore, I could not treat her to any Indian strategy.

The only chance I had was in my skill as a marksman. Realizing this, I dropped upon one knee, and raising my rifle to my shoulder, awaited her approach.

She was at this time about twenty yards away from me, advancing at a rapidly awkward and shuffling run.

I waited until she had lessened this distance probably one-half. Then, with my bead drawn behind her ear, I let her have my ball, and she dropped. It was with no small degree of pride that I contemplated her large size, for the bullet had passed through her brain, as clearly as in any shot I ever made, and she died in her tracks, mutely and gravely as any Indian brave, whose death-struggles have been chronicled by the novelist. Then, taking her two cubs under my arms, I returned to camp. Butch' skinned the grizzly. Bill on this occasion officiated as butcher. Cutting out the choicest parts of the meat, he brought them back with him. It was lucky he did so, for on visiting our traps, for the second time in that day, towards the evening, I found her bones picked tolerably clean.

Our share of the grizzly, however, lasted us for four days, and I must say, choicer meat never crossed my palate.

On our return to Honey Lake Valley, I presented one of the two cubs to Governor Roop. The other, I myself kept. At this time, it was as playful as a young kitten. Owing to its youth, I was able to thoroughly tame it, so that it would follow me wherever I went, like a spaniel. When it had increased in size to bear's estate, I made it, in after life, my constant companion. Brighton Bill gave it the name which stuck to it, of " my body-guard."

While we were upon the Humboldt, Butch' and myself had discovered what we believed to be silver ore. Brighton Bill shared our belief.

When once more near Honey Lake, we informed the various members of the Buckskin Rangers of our discovery.

All were smitten with the usual fever resulting from an intimation of the presence of either of the precious metals in any locality. It was, therefore, in the spring of 1860, that we went out and pitched our camp in a rocky defile, to which we gave the name of Prince Royal Cañon. The reason of our bestowing this title on it, will, when the date is remembered, be obvious to my readers. We were engaged " prospecting," the remainder of the spring and the succeeding summer, having located a large number of ledges.

About September we had, however, grown tired of silver-prospecting without any immediate results, and determined on adjourning our metal-mining for the winter. It was, therefore, decided that we should visit Klamath Lake and the Modoc country with the view of trapping and hunting.

We accordingly, at the commencement of the following month, struck out for the Blue Mountains, in portion of which range we pitched our camp for the purpose of looking out for good hunting-grounds. After talking the matter well over, we concluded to separate. By so doing, we could hold the whole of that portion of the country, as any good hunter and trapper can take care of ten miles square without any other help. Some of the boys accordingly went to the Klamath Lake—others betook themselves to the Sierras. In fact, they were scattered round, within no more than a day's ride of each other, while I and my pet bear, whom I had named Charley, remained on the spot we had originally camped in.

That winter set in with unusual severity. It was, indeed, the severest I had yet known, through the whole of that region.

Possibly, for twenty years, the one just past, has alone exceeded it, whether in its average temperature or the amount of the snow which fell and remained upon the earth.

In the Blue Mountains, the snow averaged from a depth of ten to eighteen feet. It covered my rude log-cabin so completely, that at times it might have been difficult for me to find it. Here it was that my bear first became of positive value to me, in addition to his affording me something like companionship.

When I left my cabin, I would leave him behind to keep house.

The result of this was, that on my return, I was sure to find him half-a-mile or more from home, to which he would pilot me unerringly.

During the night, Charley always slept with me. After building a large fire, I would lie down in his arms or rather fore-paws. He was far better than any blanket. If, however, in my sleep, the fire had gone down and the cold drove me unconsciously closer to him, than was pleasant to his Grizzlyship, he would raise his hind paw and push me into the middle of the floor. Then, it would seem as if a sense of the duty he owed his owner returned. He would roll out, himself, snuff around me, and if I kept quite still, which I have frequently done, insert his nose under my side and trundle my apparently still slumbering body back upon the bed. He possessed other qualities also, given him by nature, in which he was eminently my superior.

His hearing was wonderfully acute. Of a sudden, he would start out of the cabin, with a quick look of intelligence that was well-nigh human. After nosing around, if everything was quiet, he would slink back, with an unmistakably sheepish look. Coming up to me, he would lick my hands and face. It was precisely as if he had said:

"Don't kick up a row, old boy! I was wrong and I know it. But, it is all for the best, I should keep a bright look-out. My ears are quicker than yours, you know."

If, however, on leaving the cabin, any game, or a man should happen to be near it, he would utter a continuous low growl until I joined him.

One day he displayed his sagacity in an even stronger manner. I had gone out with my rifle in the morning and did not return until the middle of the afternoon. It was at considerably greater distance than usual from our dwelling that he met me. He would not, however, accompany me directly back, but shambled off with his rapid and swinging gait to a considerable distance. Knowing he wanted me to see something, I followed him almost as rapidly. Suddenly, he came to a dead halt. When I joined him, I learnt the reason for this strange proceeding on Charley's part. I had come upon some half-dozen or more moccasin-tracks, which led directly towards my cabin.

Of course, I now proceeded with great caution, as he also did.

About a hundred yards from the entrance, I however found precisely the same number of moccasin-tracks, bearing in an entirely different direction. They very evidently led directly from the spot to which the others had been going.

As I was examining them, his juvenile Grizzlyship lowered his quaint head above them, and as evidently scrutinized them with even greater intentness than I had done.

Then, he gave a low growl. It was exactly as if he had uttered the phrase of—

"All right!"

After this, dropping all semblance of caution, and shaking himself as a huge dog might, he shuffled off hurriedly to the hole in the snow which led to his and my habitation. When I entered it, he was circling round the whole of the somewhat narrow interior, smelling in every part, and repeating, from time to time, the low growl I have just alluded to as so significant.

It would be unnecessary to say, I did not enjoy a particularly sound slumber that night.

That the owners of these moccasins were Indians, it was impossible to doubt.

If, as some say the red men are able to do, I am unable to detect the moccasined foot-print of one tribe from that of another, I can at any rate tell whether the foot within the moccasin may chance to be a white one. These were not. Of this I had been, at once, assured.

But why had they visited my hole in the snow, and why had they afterwards left it? This last question I was unable satisfactorily to settle.

In any case, it was necessary to let the other boys know red-skins were around. Accordingly, breaking my fast early, I started towards Brighton Bill's cabin, as he was my next-door neighbor, living merely at a distance of some fifteen miles. Arriving there in the forenoon, I found him seated by a roaring fire. But scarcely had I stepped within his door, than he was on his feet with his rifle, which had been between his knees, cocked, raised, and pointed at me. It was, however, as rapidly dropped.

"By 'eaven, Mose, H'i thought you was han H'ingin."

"The Indians brought me here, Bill!"

"The blasted red devils turned hup 'ere, when H'i was hout yesterday."

"So they did, in my cabin. We ought to let the other boys know, and decide upon what had best be done."

"Butch' will be 'ere this morning. H'i seed 'im honly yesterday," said Bill. "Hif you like, H'i will go hand fetch hup some of the hother chaps."

"I think, it would be better."

"Very well, Cap! Hi'm hoff."

Putting on his snow-shoes, he started immediately.

He had scarcely left me for twenty minutes, when I heard a slight noise on the snow without. Seizing my rifle, I moved cautiously to the door, when something heavy leaped against me, which very nearly reduced me to a prostrate position. It was my bear Charley, who had thought proper to follow me. We retired within the cabin, which was considerably larger than mine. Bill was in a slight degree inclined to grandeur and luxury, if there can be such things in a log-hut. There, in company, we resigned ourselves to expectation. All at once the Grizzly raised his head. Yes! I had heard it, too. It was the movement of snow-shoes. A few moments after, Butch' entered.

On the preceding day, he also had seen Indian tracks around his dwelling.

In the afternoon, Brighton Bill reappeared. He had seen Harry Arnold, and told him to see his nearest neighbor, and send word to the other Rangers, bidding them to repair immediately to my quarters.

After a hasty feed on some jerked deer, we then set out for my dwelling. Darkness had settled on us, long before we reached it; and, but for the chilly sheen of the sheet which draped the earth with its spotless white, it might have been difficult to keep the track.

Yet I am wrong. In any case, Charley's unerring scent would have proved a sure guide. Why it was, however, I can scarcely say, save that he had confidence in our numbers, but certainly, on this occasion, he uttered no warning growl; and scarcely had we descended through the sloping snow to the doorway than two powerful arms were thrown about me. I heard Bill's voice roar:

"Look hout, Mose!"

We were in the grip of the red-skins.

The struggle was furious but brief. Our assailants had been joined by a dozen other Indians, who had been lurking without, and it was not long before we had our hands tied behind us, and we were on our way to Goose Lake.

Before starting, it must frankly be said, that with the usual red instinct for appropriating everything which comes in their way, my cabin had been thoroughly gutted. Ammunition, provision, blankets—nay, everything portable—and there was nothing which was not portable in it—had become the property of the copper-colored rascals.

Placing me in front, and Butch' and Bill behind me, in regular Indian file, they kept on either side of us, forcing us to hurry on as speedily as they could compel us to move.

It was impossible for me to forget my past experience, and I mentally resolved, if I were able to do so, that I would sell my life in square fight, rather than undergo a second time the torture to which I had then been subjected. At last, there seemed a chance for doing so. We had been compelled to move along at a smart trot for some six or seven hours, so far as I was able to measure time, when, from what cause I cannot say, although it was probably the continual friction, I felt that the ligature round my wrists was sensibly looser. My hands were able to slip through the thongs. I dared not tell either of my companions what I had done, and ask them whether or not they might be able to do the same. Some of the red rascals might understand English. One or more of them might even be renegade whites. What could I do to release them? The idea came to me like a flash of lightning. Pretending to stumble, I pitched forward, and recovering myself, got a blow on my face from one of our captors. It was apparently from one of the same thongs with which our wrists had been bound. Then, I uttered a shrill and prolonged cry as if of pain.

After this, I found myself the last of the three.

Two minutes had scarcely passed, and Bill's hands

had been freed. Mine had untied the thongs which bound them. He would have wit enough to loose Butch'. Life on the Plains and in the great West, sharpens man's mother-wit wonderfully.

Day was not yet breaking.

That heavy darkness was upon us, which so generally precedes dawn.

At this very moment we came to some low foot-hills, where the timber was dense and thick. We were obliged to move more slowly. My friends had just crossed a log, and the Indian on the left of me was stepping over it, when I fetched him with my clenched fist a violent blow under his ear. At any rate, I felt that was the place in which I struck him.

As he reeled and fell, I wrenched the gun from his hands, shouting out,

"Now's your time, boys."

The brute instinct of self-preservation answered for their closely following, without knowing that they did so, my action. In another instant we were clubbing right and left, and so soon as we could change our guns for some that had not been injured by such an employment, we commenced shooting. Scarcely had I heard the report of my first shot than I felt two vigorous arms thrown around my waist. They were lifting me from the ground, probably for the purpose of dashing me to the earth, when they suddenly relaxed their grip. A madly wild yell broke from the lips of that Indian, mingled with a ringingly fierce growl which I at once recognized, although I had never before heard it so savagely shapen, as Charley's voice.

My pet had followed on our track, and was actually assisting us in rescuing ourselves.

"My pet had followed in our track, and was actually assisting us to rescue ourselves."—*Page* 154.

Strangely enough, since the moment in which we had first found ourselves captives and were marched away in the fashion I have above described, no thought of Grizzly's absence from my side had ever crossed my mind. His memory had however been better than mine. Perhaps, when all circumstances are fairly considered, it had some reason for being so.

After a very brief struggle, the wholly unexpected assault of their three prisoners, and their four-footed or four-handed ally, on the red devils, resulted in a complete victory.

The yet living Indians cleared out, leaving us masters of the field. As the day was now gradually breaking, we were enabled to count the dead, and exercise a proprietary right in their scalps. What was of much more advantage to myself, I was enabled to recapture nearly the whole of my stolen property, as well as a number of guns, corresponding with that of the dead, which necessarily changed hands.

Eight of the scoundrels would have no more chance of troubling their white brethren.

This enumeration includes the one whom Charley had so considerately squeezed out of this life, very much, as Butch' afterwards remarked—

" As a younker squeezes a ripe orange."

It was late in the afternoon, when we arrived again at my cabin. Upon entering the hole in the snow which led to it, we found Harry Arnold, Ben Painter, and many of the boys there. They had preceded our coming by some twenty minutes. The footprints visible on the outside of my dwelling, as well as the thoroughly emptied condition of its interior, had readily given them a thorough apprehension of our condition. When we returned, they were on the point of preparing to follow on the trail of the red savages.

Of course, we had to relate our adventures since the preceding night. This, however, did not take long, as the demands of famished nature were too exacting. We had tasted neither bite nor sup since noon on the preceding day.

I may here state, that much to the mortification of Butch' and Brighton Bill, as well as somewhat to my own, it became evident that the Rangers considered my young Grizzly as the real hero of the occasion. Indeed, Painter proposed to give him a horn of old Rye, and would have done so, had I not peremptorily forbidden it, not only on the score of its possible effects upon his innocent inside, but also because our stock of that necessary article was getting very low.

After our meal, which I ate ravenously, and presume the two who had been my fellow-captives did the same, "Long" Dorsey (he stood six feet two, in his stockings) and Lute Spencer arrived. Some minutes after, we heard a voice whistling the familiar tune "Joe Bowers." This was "small" Tom Harvey, who had lingered in their rear. Seeing they had entered without exciting any commotion within the cabin, he concluded no Indians were in the immediate neighborhood. Otherwise, he would undoubtedly have refrained from allowing his lips this exercise.

We were told by Lute Spencer that they had paused at Bob Thorn's cabin by the way. He was more generally known by his intimates and associates as Dirty Bob.

"The place war gutted, as you say yours war," continued Lute, "and Bob war nowhere."

"The red devils had been there," added Dorsey. "We counted the tracks of some ten of them."

Fatigued as I was, I at once proposed starting for Bob's cabin. The memory I have already alluded to, gave me a sharp twinge of commiseration for any unlucky fellow who might be treated to a similar phase of personal experience.

CHAPTER XI.

Lots of Pluck—One of the Rangers Killed—Thinking of a Brother—Taking a Good Position—Loss of Hair, and what the Red-skins think of it—"Captain Jack's" or the Modoc Country—"Captain Jack's" Stronghold—On our Way Back—Signal-fires and Some Strategy—Half a Hundred Scalps for One—The Pah-utes on the War-path—Fishing for the Dead—The White Flag—Washo Bravery.

Bob's location was at some thirty miles' distance from my cabin, and we arrived there, shortly after the dazzling rays of the morning sun were blindingly increased in strength by the reflection from the snow.

Spencer and Dorsey had told us the bare fact. Butch', however, had a keener nose than they apparently possessed.

"Dirty Bob fit well for it," he said, after glancing through the cabin. " Some of the red skunks war hurt, and no mistake. He al'ays had lots o' pluck."

He was unmistakably right. There were marks of blood on the hard soil of the floor. But, whether the soaked in and dead crimson had once run in his veins or those of his Indian enemies, remained to be seen. We almost at once struck their trail, which led through the forest, beyond the spot he had selected for his hunting-ground. This we followed, for something more than six miles. The track was by no means an easy one, rising and falling, broken up by rocks and intersected with the stumps of fallen trees. In short, it was one which none of the delicate nurslings of city civilization would have cared about following, even for the purpose of pulling trigger at their first live venison, and, of necessity, missing it.

Arnold and Painter were in advance.

The fatigue of the past two days and night had kept me somewhat in the rear of the party, with Butch' and "Fatty."

Painter uttered a savage oath.

We ran up to him. He and Arnold were standing close to the body of poor Bob. His knife, smeared with dried or frozen blood, was still clenched in the hands of the corpse, which was frightfully mutilated. It had also been scalped. Evidently, his death had been the result of a vigorous struggle to escape; for the snow on which he was lying was crushed in and trodden down in every direction; while a young tree had been torn from its roots by the force with which some one had fallen against it. Glancing at Ben Painter, I saw that his teeth were set tightly together, and his under lip, which his beard permitted me to see, was rigid and almost blue. I took him by the hand and squeezed it.

"I war thinking of my brother."

This was all he said, as we continued upon the trail.

From this point, it could very readily be followed. The marks of blood were visible enough all along it. One or more of the red-skins had been wounded. In about half a mile further, the road became easier and the trees were more scattered. Arnold, who was still in front with Painter, and Brighton Bill, had sighted what they supposed to be a dead Indian.

"Here's one of them," cried Arnold.

Scarcely had he uttered this than, wounded as he was, the savage leapt to his feet and ran. His strength, however, only availed him for a short spurt. He again dropped, and, while on the ground, drew his bow. The arrow struck Bill on the left arm, making a slight flesh wound. But before the red devil could discharge another, Ben Painter was up with him, and the knife he had drawn was buried in his heart. On examining the dead body, we discovered the wound Bob had inflicted on its side. Blood was still slowly oozing from it.

From this point, the trail diverged towards the Lower Klamath Lake. We followed on it as rapidly as possible, passing Shasta Mountain, until we arrived at Fall River. Beyond this stream lies the country, which is the stronghold of the Modoc and Pit-River tribes.

It is certainly a fitting section to have such an appellation applied to it.

Throughout, it is covered with natural fortifications. Huge rocks rise from the earth, varying from two hundred to three hundred and fifty feet in height. A single precipitous and narrow path, sometimes natural, not unfrequently fashioned by the Modocs or their tributaries, the Pit-River Indians, who are by no means as warlike, leads to the top of these. Here, in many cases, the summit is defended by a breastwork. In the beds of lava, for this part of the country has formerly been volcanic, you will also occasionally come upon a triangle of rocks, from four to six feet in height, with a steep cavity in their centre, large enough in every case to admit a man, and frequently much larger. The reasons of these curious formations I leave to more inquiringly scientific minds than my own. They are certainly too numerous, as well as now too low, to be supposed the series of small craters from which lava formerly flowed.

Even in saying this, I feel I am getting beyond my depth.

Let me, therefore, confine myself to the details of actions which I am assuredly able to speak of, from the mere fact that I very decidedly took part in them.

We had followed the Modocs as far as Battle Creek.

Here, knowing the situation they intended to trap us into, we halted for two days, in order to give ourselves some rest, and enable a portion of the Rangers whom our speed had outstripped to catch up with us.

On the second day we consulted together for a long time. This council was the first in which my advice had not been immediately taken by the Rangers, without any opposition.

It was, that we should make what a military tactician would call a feint.

In other words, we should seem to retire as if we did not dare to carry the pursuit any further. During the succeeding night we might return, and, under its cover, secure one of the best positions in the section of country immediately beyond Fall River.

Harry Arnold and Lute Spencer decidedly objected to this. They asserted that it would be the first time in which we had ever backed from any number of the "darned red skunks." Many of the others agreed with them, amongst whom were Butch' and "Fatty."

Painter, however, greatly to my surprise, in the teeth of their opposition, took my side of the question, as did Brighton Bill. Laying his broad hand on my shoulder, the latter said:

"The Cap's more nor 'arf ha Hinjun. Hi'll be blamed hif 'e hisn't right!"

At length we carried the day, and broke up our camp

on the following morning. Upon the same night we returned, moving with the greatest silence and caution, securing a position admirably adapted for my purpose. Part of the Rangers took possession of one of the natural forts which commanded an area of some two hundred yards in width. The rest of us were posted in a series of the triangular pits opposite this position. Their duty was similar to that of sharpshooters, although I may say not a single Ranger would have been unfit for such a duty, or would have failed in it.

It was a little after daybreak, when we first caught sight of a party of the Modocs. These counted barely ten. They had evidently come out to see whether we had quitted our late position by Battle Creek.

Nothing was to be seen of us. The Creek was visible. Consequently returning, they halted immediately between the rock on which part of our number were encamped and the rifle-pits opposite. From this spot they despatched a runner to warn the remainder of the redskins. So far, everything had worked rightly. In some twenty minutes more fifty or sixty of the remaining Modocs had joined their scouting party.

They were together, some pointing in the direction they supposed us to have taken, and others talking, it may be presumed, on the wisdom of following us, when I gave the word.

We all had Sharp's carbines. Indeed, these were our invariable fighting weapons. Throwing in cartridge after cartridge, we kept up an almost continuous fire. Those who escaped our balls, scattered in every possible direction.

Forty-three of the red-skins had been slain.

After taking their scalps, we started off in the direction of Pit River.

Here, possibly, the reader may feel some shrinking horror at the constant repetition made by me, of this, to his mind, unpleasantly barbaric proceeding. Let him remember that the unscalped Indian is supposed, by his red brethren, to hold a higher rank in the Happy Hunting Grounds of his belief than the one who has lost his hair. He will then form some idea of the reason for which the white ranger or scout invariably scalps the red-skin who has fallen under his ball.

When we were near old Fort Crook, a signal-fire was seen, far to our left.

Having advised with Arnold, he and Bill ascended the mountain nearest us, to answer it from that point. Crossing the valley to the further side, I repeated the answering signal from the opposite hill. Then, passing the low "divide" or range of insignificantly steep ground between Pit and Fall Rivers, we once more started a signal-fire, on the highest point we could find.

All that seemed at the moment left for us to do, was to conceal ourselves and wait what might next turn up. While hidden, Brighton Bill touched my arm.

"Hi'm blamed hif the red rascals harn't hat hit hagain."

His eyes had been quicker than mine or any of the rest of us. Another signal had been kindled on a large bald or bare mountain on our left, and slightly in our rear. Butch' was sent to a hill lying some half of a mile to our right, to answer this. He was one of the quietest scouts amongst the Rangers; and saying this, is paying him a high compliment, when all of us had learnt to be so apt and ready. He had been, on this occasion, selected by me, because the last signal-fire had ignited so near to us, that caution and care were absolutely necessary in him who replied to it, to prevent any detection of the white man who might be employed to kindle it. We waited for his reply some time. Almost immediately after it was seen by us, the smoke from an answer to it was seen upon a low hill to the right of our ambuscade. There was certainly no possibility of mistaking the meaning of this signal. It was an inquiry whether the friends who had so kindly answered them were "on our trail?"

We were waiting for Hasbrouck to come back, when we saw in the gathering gloom the crimson light of another signal-fire, farther up the valley.

Without coming back for new orders, Butch' had exercised his own judgment. He had displayed his rapidity of decision and accuracy of calculation, in what he had done.

He had not yet returned when I saw a party of Indians, numbering in all, from twenty to twenty-five, stringing, with great care and silence, up the valley. Quite unconscious of our ambush, they advanced right into it.

But, that the boys fired too soon, not a single one of the luckless red-skins would have escaped.

As it was, eight of them paid the penalty of having mistaken our signal-fires for those of their own friends. In almost a word, I may say that the slaughter of fifty-one Modocs had atoned for the death of our luckless associate, Bob Thorn.

His was the first name wiped out from the Buckskin Rangers, and, after we had punished the tribe which had taken his life, not unnaturally, his memory was frequently recalled by most of us, with sorrow.

I was possibly the only one of the Rangers that remembered the close of his life, with something approaching pleasure. The dead man had been enabled by it, to escape that most horrible of dooms, as I was too well aware, the slow death at the stake.

About the end of February, we once more reached the settlement at the lower end of Honey Lake. We were enabled to carry with us a fair stock of skins, or as the traders call them, " peltry."

These we disposed of at a reasonable and remunerative figure. No sooner had we done so, than after a few days' idleness spent with friends and acquaintances, the larger part of us decided upon returning to our silver lodes upon the Humboldt River. The truth is, that during the past fall and winter, the report of our success in prospecting for ore in that locality, had spread far and wide. It had exercised the usual charm which the news of such a discovery invariably does. If we had delayed in the occupancy of our claims, we might, in the sequel, have found them a subject of dispute. The law of the mines is an unwritten one. Consequently, its strictness in some points is only equalled by its vagueness in others. Here our luck was various enough, but on the whole we fairly prospered. Nothing of particular account, however, presents itself for me to put on record, save the presence of my friends and his Grizzlyship, my now considerably large pet, Charley.

On returning from our life at these mines, we spent the whole of the following winter in the valley or at Susanville.

It would be useless to inquire into the reason of our doing so. Possibly we were lazy, or more probably had reaped too much profit from mining and trapping, during the past year. However, there were no Indian troubles that season. There may be an equal chance that this was the reason of our comparative inactivity.

The succeeding winter, that of 1861 and '62, will be remembered by all old Californians as one of the most severe which had ever occurred in that part of our country. The mountains were closed very early, so early, indeed, that few or none of the settlers in the up-lands had got in their winter supplies. They were actually shut in by the heavy snow-falls, from the possibility of doing so.

In addition to this trouble, our old enemies, the Pah-ute Indians, had again become restless.

Possibly, Uncle Sam had forgotten to purchase their forbearance. At any rate, they were again upon the war-path, for the purpose of stealing stock.

My first knowledge of this arose from the following occurrence:

A lame man, named Thomas Bear, was at this period keeping the Deep Hole Spring Station, on the Humboldt road. He chanced to be in the valley upon business, when some travellers from the Humboldt passed through it, on their way to Susanville. In passing Deep Hole, they had paused at the Station. It was to find it deserted and plundered of almost everything which an Indian would be likely to take. The floor was marked with numerous stains of blood, and there were unmistakable signs visible, which clearly told them a savage struggle had recently taken place there. Meeting Tom, they recounted these facts to him.

He had known me for some three years, and hunting me up—for if anywhere in this end of Honey Lake Valley, no man was very difficult to find,—asked me to accompany him to the Station, to discover what was the matter. The request was a natural one, and I at once complied with it.

From snow the roads were almost impassable, save on foot. I, nevertheless, set out with my lame companion on this pleasant tramp.

While resting during the night at George Laithrop's Ranch, as a matter of course, I explained the facts which induced me to accompany Bear. A young lad no more than sixteen years of age overheard me, and wished to go with us. In fact, he displayed such a determination to make a third in our party, that I could not refuse him.

"You must get a rifle from Laithrop," I said, when he asked me to take him with us.

"I've one of my own, and a Colt's six-mouthed barker, too," was his reply.

"If so, you can come with us."

On the next morning, we started again, Tom, the boy, and myself. Little trouble was anticipated by me from the red-skins, in spite of what Bear had heard. The road from the Humboldt was so constantly travelled over, and lay so much out of the usual line of their depredations, that I was almost disinclined to put full faith in the account which he had so implicitly accepted. Mud Spring Station had, however, been apparently abandoned, and we were compelled to push on to Smoke Creek without resting there. Next day, we rose early, and made the best speed we could, in the hope of reaching Deep Hole on the same night. This was, however, in consequence of the depth of the snow in many places, impossible. We were forced to stop at Wall Springs. This was at six miles' distance from the point to which our steps were directed.

When, on the succeeding day, shortly after dawn, we arrived at the Station, we found that the travellers had told Tom nothing but the truth.

Nevertheless, on a thorough examination, I found that none of the provisions or blankets had been taken. Nothing but the guns and ammunition had been made away with. But for the marks of blood on the floor and in the doorway, it is more than probable Bear's suspicions might have been equally divided between the man he had left in charge of the Station and the red-skins.

As yet, nothing had been found inside the premises to indisputably settle the fact of the man's murder, or if he had been murdered, to prove how or by whom the outrage had been committed.

The snow in front of the house might possibly have offered some proof; but the feet of the party who had brought the news to Honey Lake, had effaced all such evidence, which might have been left on it. Some days had, to a certainty, elapsed. My life in the last few years had, however, taught me the two great Indian virtues, patience and persistence. Only half of our search was yet over.

I began to examine the grounds round the Station, and found, leading to one of the largest and deepest of the springs from which it has taken its name, the track of moccasins.

Getting a long *lariat*, which lame Tom had procured for me, I extemporized a hook from the hoop of an old keg, and with the line to which I had attached it, began fishing in the spring, for anything I might find in it.

Nor, was my search long unrewarded.

Shortly after, in dragging the bottom, my hook caught hold of something heavy. When we had raised it to the surface of the water, it proved to be a body. As I glanced at Bear, he said, with almost a groan:

"Sure enough, it's poor Dave."

The head of the murdered man had been split with a hatchet, and afterwards scalped. A fragment of rock had been tied to the body by the Pah-utes for the purpose of sinking it.

After we had interred it, as decently as we could, we proceeded to *cachè* the blankets, provisions, and anything else which might be of value. All of the stock had been driven off, with the exception of a lame horse. This we took away with us, as, otherwise, it must have perished.

On our return, when we had reached the low Sand Hills at the foot of Smoke-creek Cañon, we saw eight or ten red-skins coming down the side of the mountain to the right of the track in front of us. Each of them carried a stick with a piece of white rag tied to it. In the hands of an Indian, a flag of any sort means fight, and we knew it. Our preparations were speedily made. Telling the boy to lead the horse and draw his revolver, I gave his rifle to Tom Bear, who had none, bidding him cover our rear. Then, before taking my place in front, an uncommon one for most generals, and only to be pardoned on account of the exceedingly restricted number of my army, I gave my directions to the boy. They were very simple. He was to follow after me, and not use his Colt, unless I fired—if necessitated to do so.

When all was settled satisfactorily, we steadily advanced.

Soon after, the Washos reached the road. So, at least, my lame friend afterwards said they were, and it appears probable, as ten Pah-utes to two whites and a boy, even if a tall one, would scarcely have been cowed so easily. They had drawn up on either side of the track, and attempted to induce us to stop. Pushing them right and left with my rifle, I paid no attention to this, and as soon as we had passed, faced round, bidding Tom to do the same, until we were out of the range of their arrows. None of them had fire-arms.

On reaching the cañon, instead of going through it, we crossed to the west side, in the view of preventing any risk of an ambush from them while we were in the defile. Had we exposed ourselves to this chance, and had they enough resolution to have availed themselves of it, their arrows would have told, while, unless they had incautiously uncovered themselves, there would have been exceedingly small risk of their losing any of their own party. Tom Bear was right. They very certainly could not have been Pah-utes.

We had no more trouble until we reached Laithrop's Ranch, which we did in as short a period as lame Tom and the still lamer quadruped could traverse the distance. Here, the lad who had accompanied us was to remain; and when I left him there, I was unable to refrain from giving him a few words of warm praise.

"You behaved very well, my boy, when you gave up your rifle, at once. If you obey orders so promptly now, some day you will be in a position to give them."

"I'm right glad, Captain Mose, to hear you tell me that."

As he said this, the young fellow flushed through his richly bronzed skin up to the very roots of his hair, with pleasure.

When I saw him, a somewhat sad and bitter reflection came over me. In the far West, self-reliance comes early as well as quickly. Manhood grows with action, not by years. How soon, life must rob him of the capacity of blushing at any such recognition of obedience.

There, amid the roughly hardy dwellers on the frontier, exertion rapidly blots out the modest valuation of our own merits. It, indeed, teaches a self-appreciation which frequently approaches the style of Bombastes, and which I have not uncommonly heard stigmatized as braggadocio.

This is, nevertheless, an unfair judgment. He who has to be ready for anything, whose energy and audacity have drawn him through difficulties and dangers his Eastern fellow-countryman never has been exposed to, will at times necessarily glorify his own pluck and endurance. And why should he not do so, having none around him who would be inclined to sing his praises, while they believe themselves equally or more gallant and plucky than he is?

CHAPTER XII.

DANGER IN THE AIR—THE CHOICE OF A CAPTAIN—AN EFFECTUAL SARCASM—GOING LAME—"THE HEATHEN CHINEE"—A MILITARY ENGINEER WITHOUT A COMMISSION—NO VENTILATION—SMOTHERING LIKE RATS IN A HOLE—THE MOMENTARY SURPRISE—TWO RED-SKINS—LEAVING THEIR GUNS OUTSIDE—TRAPPED—"THE HEATHEN CHINEE" ONCE MORE—SOME QUIET TALK.

THE next two or three weeks passed, to all appearance, quietly enough. There was, however, an unpleasant feeling in Susanville and around Honey Lake, of danger in the air. Perhaps, this feeling was not wholly unpleasant. The Rangers had now been idle for a tolerably long time. That is to say, there had recently been no positive Indian troubles.

However, the Deep Hole Spring murder had sounded the preparatory note.

Not long afterwards the gathering storm broke on us. A large stock of cattle belonging to Bill Long and Allen Wood had been in the charge of five good and trusty *Buccahros* or herdsmen, at the upper end of the valley. But red cunning, in this case, baffled white honesty. One dark night, three hundred head of stock were driven off; and in the morning the herdsmen found themselves without any herd to look after. At the time when the intelligence reached it, I was in Susanville. In less than an hour after we heard the facts, the Rangers, with the exception of three, were in the saddle, and on their way to Emmerson's Ranch, from which the cattle had been driven. Two of the three we picked up on the road there. The third overtook us, long before we had arrived at the spot where our services were required.

About fifty volunteers had collected at the Ranch, when we reached it. They were occupied in the momentous duty of choosing a captain, and appeared to find no small difficulty in making their selection. As soon as Harry Arnold appreciated this difficulty, he approached me with an air of very far profounder respect than he had ever before exhibited to me, and raising his hand to his forehead in soldier-like style, said with great gravity:

"Captain! Don't you think we had better take the trail? They won't have chosen their commanding officer until—"

"The Day hof Judgment!" broke in Brighton Bill, with an oath.

"And after that," continued Harry with the same imperturbable seriousness, "they will have to elect a Lieutenant, a Sergeant, and—"

"'Alf ha dozen Horderlies!"

For once in my life I very nearly forgot duty, as I looked at the two whose criticism on the election going on, was couched in styles so widely opposed. To avoid roaring with laughter, I roared out in a very different tone.

"Rangers! take the trail."

In another instant, we were following its sufficiently broad and plain indication.

Let me, as we pursue it, mention that Harry Arnold's gentlemanly reproof, and Bill's coarser satire produced an immediate result. David Blanchard was chosen captain of the Volunteers, in less than five minutes, and in no more than ten after we were on the trail, they also were in the saddles, and following it, closely behind us.

Blanchard had lived on the Plains for years, and was in every respect well adapted for his present position. We soon had a good understanding, and when we arrived at Smoke Creek where the Indians had evidently camped for the night, on the day before, a plan of action was agreed upon.

The horses were accordingly sent back under a sufficient guard to the Ranch, and we divided ourselves into two parties. One of these was to follow the red robbers up Painter's Cañon, which direction they had taken. The other was to continue down Smoke Creek, by Buffalo Springs, to protect the settlers from any other bands of the Pah-utes which might be out, after anything they could pick up—provision or stock, weapons or lives.

Very unfortunately, shortly after we had started, John Partridge and myself, with one of the pack-horses retained to carry blankets and provisions, as well as a Chinese who had accompanied the volunteers as a man of all work, became so lame that it was impossible for us to continue at the same speed as the rest of the party.

It was a matter of obvious necessity, that we should give up all idea of doing so.

In consequence of this, Arnold took my place in command of the Rangers, and with a sore heart in one bosom at least, I turned my back upon the men whose labors and dangers I had so long partaken. It would be almost impossible for me to explain precisely what my feelings were at that moment. Of course, I felt none who had shared my previous struggles would impute my disability to anything approaching fear, or a disinclination to endure privation. And yet, in the immediate pursuit of the rascals who had plundered two of our prominent settlers, I was compelled to leave it entirely to others. In my eyes, this almost seemed a humiliation which it must be long before I could surmount, and which subsequent toil and courage might alone wipe out.

Necessarily, this now appears childish to myself as it will doubtless to my readers. However, I felt it, and my heart seemed to weep tears of blood and shame as I did so.

We had determined upon returning through Rush Valley, for two reasons. One of them was, that knowing the ground, we fancied it would be easier to travel for us in our partially disabled condition. The other was even a simpler one. On reaching Mud Springs, which even in our present state we might fairly count upon doing by nightfall, we should find a resting place. This was in the house of a man whom I knew tolerably well, and who had formerly kept the Station at this place.

Upon reaching Mud Springs, which we did earlier than we had calculated on doing, we repaired to his dwelling, where we were welcomed warmly.

Scarcely, however, had he placed food before us, with some capital coffee, than he began questioning us about the Indians. He asked us what we had heard of them—whether they were yet moving—what action had been taken with regard to them, and lastly, how it was that I, Buckskin Mose, as I was now generally called, chanced to be here? In reply, I recounted to him the plunder of Emmerson's Ranch, of which, he had as yet heard nothing, and the steps which had been taken to pursue the Pah-ute thieves. My narration was concluded with, I fear, no peculiarly pious expression of pleasure at having been compelled to leave the Rangers at a time when I should so desire to have been at their head.

As he listened to what I was saying, he chuckled audibly, and seeing my look of astonishment, afterwards explained what had induced him to indulge in so strange an exhibition of merriment.

"Yer see, Cap! I'm ready for 'em if they look me up. I don't choose to turn tail, like some of my neighbors."

"What do you mean?"

"I was sartain the copper-colored devils were preparing for something o' the sort, and so made a hole under the chapparal behind the house, whar I don't much think they'll spot me, when I take to it."

The hole he alluded to was a large and comfortable excavation conducted to by a subterranean passage of considerable length. It had taken him several weeks to dig out the passage and room, which last was sufficiently spacious to *cachè* all his goods, and even portion of his stock, if the necessity of doing so was forced upon him. He exhibited his fortification, or we should perhaps call it his citadel, to myself, Partridge, and the Chinaman, with a good deal of pride.

Nor, indeed, was it a place of security to be laughed at, by a solitary dweller on the frontier during Indian troubles. Nature had evidently not dealt on the square with him. With the advantages of education, the fellow would have made a good military engineer.

Fatigued with our day's tramp, we retired at an early hour, and had been asleep but a short time, when we were aroused by the continual barking of his two watch-dogs. These, I had noticed on arriving at the house. They were noble-looking animals.

Throwing aside my blanket, and sitting up, I noticed that Partridge had done the same.

As for the person who had failed to find his natural avocation, he was already on his feet, as also was our Chinese friend. The latter volunteered a very unnecessary explanation.

"Doggee too much barkee. Pig-tail Bobbee, no sleepee."

The dogs certainly did keep up a confounded row. We concluded that, under the circumstances, a renewed attempt at slumber would be useless. In accordance with this view of the situation, John Partridge and myself also rose, "keeping an eye out" for what might turn up next.

We had only been on our legs for a few minutes, when one of the dogs rushed against the door with a prolonged howl. On opening it, he ran in, and we saw an arrow sticking in his body. The door was instantly closed and barred. It was clear that we were attacked, and I instantly peered through one of the small holes with which the boarded and sodded walls of the house were pierced, to see what I could.

It was dark enough. Yet my eyes were sufficiently keen to discern the dusky forms of objects moving in front, which were evidently red-skins.

But the gloom was too great for us to fire with a reasonable chance of hitting them. We must wait for the daylight. It was now some two hours past midnight, and when the dawn broke we should—ha! what was this? Smoke driving through the dried sods on the inside of the walls, followed here and there, where the shrinking of the matted earth had given such a chance, by lancing tongues of flame.

Light had been afforded us much sooner than we had, in any way, anticipated.

The red devils had set the house on fire.

It was clear that we should have to abandon our outer works, and retire into the stronghold.

We accordingly made an orderly retreat through the tunnel which has already been mentioned, carrying all our ammunition and weapons with us. The Pah-utes had of course expected us to attempt an escape above ground. In that case, they would have been able, by the light of the blazing dwelling, to have counted us out and raised our hair. As it was, we preferred concealing ourselves under the earth. This enabled us to save our scalps, at any rate, for the time.

We had carried a spade with us. It was necessary to fill up the passage through which we quitted the burning dwelling. In any less pressing necessity than the present, I should certainly have set Pig-tail Bobbee at the work of closing it. Chinese labor, however, although thorough, is by no means rapid enough in moments of necessity.

So, I began it. Partridge and the engineer followed. Each worked in turn, almost as fast as chain lightning.

In some ten or twelve minutes the mouth of the narrow tunnel was blocked up, I may honestly say, with a speed and completeness which even a Brunel or a Stephenson would have appreciated. McClellan would have been nowhere, if his work had been brought into comparison with ours on the score of rapidity.

We then transferred ourselves to the citadel. As I before intimated, it was sufficiently large. However, it possessed one inconvenience with regard to John and myself.

The engineer was a short man. He had dug it out, with an eye to his own convenience. The Chinaman was even shorter. Consequently, he also found it lofty enough for his height. But we counted nearly six feet in stature. However, in such a case as the present one, minor personal discomforts had to be overlooked. A graver one now presented itself. The engineer had provided no means of ventilation. We had tenanted the internal fort for some half an hour, when the atmosphere became unpleasantly close. It might even have been pronounced stifling. Some means of procuring fresh air had at once to be found. I questioned our friend as to the presumable distance between the top of my skull and the bottom of the *chapparal*.

" Tain't far, Cap, atween one and the other," was his answer.

" How far? "

" Mebbee, six inches," he reflectively answered.

" You're sure of that? "

" Or mebbee, six foot! "

" Good Heavens! man, have you no clearer idea about it than that? "

" How on airth should I, Cap? "

" Don't you know that there's a good chance of our being smothered, like rats in a hole which has been stopped up? "

" Yow could I help it? "

There was no use in discussing the subject with the luckless engineer. That was evident. Something, however, had to be done, and very shortly. A rat in such a case would use its teeth without pausing to discuss how much or how little he had to gnaw through. My teeth were not exactly adapted to such an experiment. But my ramrod might be a good probe, and if it found bottom or top (which it was, it would have been difficult to say) the spade might save us.

In another instant I was working my ramrod through the earthen roof of our air-tight, although scarcely pregnable citadel.

The earth was soft, and in less than a minute I felt its end had reached fresh air, although none of that desirable commodity had yet reached us. In order to enlarge the hole I had made, I was working the slip of wrought-iron with which I had produced it, round and round, when a large piece of rock fell down from the side of it, with a quantity of loose soil.

It scraped my shoulder.

"What tumblee?" screamed Pig-tail Bobby.

"Hold your tongue, you fool!" said Partridge. "Don't you feel, Mose has saved us from stifling."

With the fresh air, a little light, it was very little, came through the hole to us. As for me, I felt a new man. Looking around for a barrel which I had seen in the excavation when we had first visited it, with its proprietor, I set it erect under the ventilator so unexpectedly manufactured. Mounting on it, I protruded my head through the bottom of the *chapparal.* Day had already broken. Through the under branches of the trees I could see the still smoking timbers of the burned-down house. The rascally Pah-utes were dancing around them, in fiendish glee.

It was too great a temptation to be resisted, and I asked John to hand me my rifle.

After he had handed it to me, I passed its barrel through the bushes with great care, so as to avoid any noise which might attract the attention of the Indians.

Never, possibly, was any red devil more surprised than that Pah-ute, when he felt the leaden messenger of death crashing through his skull.

His surprise, however, was but momentary. It silenced him forever.

They handed me another rifle, and another of the red-skins fell.

Yet another, and another—until, at last, when nine of the Indians had been slain, the remainder of them fled from the scene they had so recently fancied one of complete victory.

We now quitted the cave which had served us so well, having taken some pork from the barrel I had used to stand upon with so much advantage. While cooking this on the still burning embers of the house, I saw the charred carcase of the poor hound, who had given us so timely a warning. He had been forgotten by his master, when we took refuge in the citadel, constructed by him without the indispensable requisite of an air-hole.

As we were drinking a little sugarless and milkless coffee, chancing to turn my head, I saw something moving in a large sage-brush.

Leaping to my feet, I started for it, and as I did so an Indian broke from it and ran. He did this in a zigzag manner, leaping from side to side, which rendered it a matter of extreme difficulty to fetch him. At length, however, I was enabled to accomplish this. He must have been on a scouting expedition from the party we had so narrowly escaped. If so, he had not well calculated the time of his return. Half an hour later or earlier, he might have kept his scalp.

Although still lame, I was enabled to cover more ground on our way back to the Ranch of George Laithrop, which we arrived at, close upon four o'clock in the afternoon.

A little after we had entered it, and while we were eating our supper, Laithrop, who had been out when we got there, turned up. He was astonished to see me, supposing I had been with the Rangers; but he had little time to devote to the expression of any such feeling. Two mounted Pah-utes were advancing to the house. Three months since they would have been received as friends, so far at least as a red-skin can ever be deemed friendly by the white man, of whom, on the slightest chance or whim, he is ready to become the enemy. After the preceding few days, they could merely be regarded in the light of the latter designation.

"Let them enter, Laithrop! but without their guns. We will go into the back-room."

In two or three minutes the red-skins were at the door. He told them, they must "leave" their "guns outside." They were probably upon an expedition for spying out the nakedness of the land, and counted on doing no immediate harm, as they consented to do this. Leaning one gun on either side of the door, they accordingly entered the main-room of the Ranch. Partridge and myself quitted the house by the rear doorway, and passing round it on either side, secured their two weapons. Having effected this, I entered the room, followed by my companion, and told them they were "our prisoners." An indescribable mixture of rage and fear flashed over the features of the taller red-skin.

"The Pah-ute know Buckskin Mose. He laugh at his words, a heap."

While saying this, he had leapt into a corner of the room, caught up an old repeating rifle which was standing there, and struck heavily with it at George Laithrop. Had Laithrop not dodged the blow, it would have severely injured him. As it was, it caught him slantwise on the back and sent him staggering across the room.

The next instant he was struggling with myself and Partridge.

He managed to draw his knife.

However, this had been seen by me in time to avoid the thrust. With a blow from my fist, I dashed him from me. At the same instant a shot from his own Minie rifle, which Laithrop had caught up from the place where I had laid it, passed through his breast, and he fell.

Then I looked round for his companion.

To my surprise, I found him on the bed in the grip of Pig-tail Bobby. Never before had I seen a Chinaman with any fight in him. It was my first experience of a new phase in the character of the "Heathen Chinee." Bobby's knife was out, and in another minute the Pah-ute's life-blood would have been staining the blankets. This was a most useless proceeding, as blankets, at this time, were not over-plentiful round Honey Lake. Therefore I pulled Pig-tail back, with a round exclamation of disgust at the lavish profligacy of such a proceeding.

The red-skin, however, had more leg and less pluck

than his companion. Leaping from the bed, he darted through the door, and was off.

However, I was as quick as he was. No sooner had I seen him make for the open, than I was after him. As I left the house I had caught up a double-barrelled shot-gun, and brought him down before he had run fifty yards from it.

After burying the Indians, Partridge started with me for Susanville, taking their ponies with us.

A few days only had passed when Harry Arnold also returned with the rest of the Rangers. They had recaptured only a few head of cattle. The rest of the herd had been killed by the thieving red-skins, in the same cowardly manner which I have elsewhere detailed.

One might have fancied the lesson they had received at Mud Springs, and the close pursuit which had induced their main body to resort to this expedient, would have kept them quiet. It, however, did not. The periodical lust for robbery and bloodshed which seems, from time to time, to possess them, had mastered their nature. More complete punishment could alone stop it.

A week later, George Laithrop sent me a pressing demand to come down with a few of the boys and pass some time with him. Two Pah-utes had recently appeared at the Ranch, and told him they had seen Buckskin Mose and himself kill their two companions and bury them. They had then threatened him with prompt vengeance, openly telling him that they intended not only to kill him and burn his house in a few days, but to slaughter every white man in the valley.

It must be owned that the open hardihood of these threats looked ominous. The red-skin so seldom threatens before he strikes, that it seemed to me the dwellers about the Lake might be exposed to a graver danger from the Indians, than any they had as yet incurred.

In consequence of this belief, my men were at once summoned. The same day we started for George's Ranch, and got there after nightfall. On consulting with Laithrop, it was considered advisable to keep the Rangers as much out of sight as possible, to prevent the red-skins from realizing how well he was protected. In compliance with this idea, only some half-dozen of the boys, amongst whom was Tom Harvey and myself, became occupants of the house. Half of the remainder were stationed in a large log *corral* about one hundred yards distant on the south side. The rest were secreted in an old root-shed, or rather in the cellar of one, to the west.

George and myself sat by the burning logs on his hearth, talking on until a late hour.

Our subject was the red man, and he bitterly denounced the way in which our Government dealt with such a grave subject. It was, he said, continually patting them on the back, and buying a temporary truce. This, he believed, made the Indians actually think that a power which had only to plant its heel firmly upon them and crush them out of existence, actually feared their strength. "Greater liars, more unblushing thieves, as well as more reckless murderers," he continued, never existed. And these were the men whom Uncle Sam protected against his own children, whenever the blue-coats appeared upon the frontier.

Nor can I affirm but that he is, in the main, right. It is only by terrible punishment for their crimes, the whites are able to keep the red-skins within anything like reasonable bounds.

My knowledge of them, up to this time, vouched for the necessity of such retaliation. In no case which I have yet recounted had the settlers commenced an Indian war, if these struggles are entitled to such a name. When we struck, the blow was called for, by gross outrage or bloodier murder. Since I had met and known them, I had encountered no red-skin who had dealt squarely with me, except the father of Clo-ke-ta and Old Spotted Tail. And, possibly, of all the tribes I had yet any acquaintance with, the Pah-utes possessed the fewest virtues and the most thorough vices. George Laithrop's opinion of the Indian, founded in a great measure upon their character, was, in a fuller or lesser degree, shared by all who had ever been brought in contact with them.

CHAPTER XIII.

A Little Compassion—White Folly and Red Treachery—
A Squeak for Life—Making Tracks—Female Society—
A Taste of Western Civilization—Deferring a Honeymoon—The Army Officer—Trailing and Spotting—A
Chance to look at a little Indian Fighting—Wrathful and Righteous Buncombe—Forced to Bend One's
Head—Mirth even at the Point of Death.

We had not to wait long for the red-skins to attempt carrying out their late threats. On this occasion, we also had a good example afforded us of their gratitude, and keen sense of obligation for kindness.

About ten o'clock on the following day, I discovered some thirty-five or forty of them descending the side of the mountain near the Ranch, on their ponies. Tom Harvey was at the moment standing by me. He recognized an Indian at their head whom he had almost, as he himself expressed it, raised. He had lived with Tom for several years, and on one occasion, had saved Tom's life. Naturally enough, old love for the lad, who was now barely eighteen years of age, moved Harvey's bowels strongly with compassion.

Being, as my readers already know, a largely fat man, his compassion for the young Pah-ute was as oilily large and full-sized.

To state matters briefly, he wished to save him, and applied to me for permission to go out and warn him to leave.

"If I grant it, you must keep your tongue still, upon our being here."

"In course I will, Cap!"

"Not one word must you utter about our presence at the Ranch."

"D' yer think I'm a fool, Cap?"

Well! It can be no use to induce the belief that I did not wish him to go. Perhaps, at the time, owing to my conversation with Laithrop on the night before, I may have fancied we had judged the red rascals too harshly. Possibly—but there is no reason for my hesitation, or beating the cover. I may as well have it out, at once. The truth is, like an idiot, I permitted him to constitute himself good adviser to the one red-skin in particular, and necessarily to the others in general.

With my full sympathy he walked towards the Indians, and motioned to him he had recognized, to come forward. The young Pah-ute advanced.

Tom spoke to him, and the red-skin replied, making a gesture of dissent as he did so. After this Harvey continued long and earnestly, apparently urging him warmly to induce his colored friends to desist from their hostile intentions. The Indian, with an emphatic movement of the arm, seemed positively to refuse attempting to bring them to any such concession. It was then I saw the Ranger point in the direction of the *corral* in which I had stationed portion of my men.

Immediately that I saw this, I became aware of the folly I had been guilty of, even more clearly than Harvey himself, soon afterwards, was of his

The young red-skin turned at once to his companions, pointing to the *corral*, and uttering a few rapid words. Then I saw Tom Harvey rushing back towards me, while the Pah-utes fired a volley on the house or shed to which the Ranger's insane frankness had directed them. It was merely made of boards, an inch in thickness, reared end-ways. Their bullets riddled it, with the rattle of a storm of hail. All we could do in return was to fire on them from the *corral* and the house, as they turned tail and urged their ponies up the mountain they had been descending. We saw five or six of them reel in their saddles. But they were prevented from falling from them, by their companions, until the whole of them were out of sight.

One of our own men had been instantly killed by their volley.

My wish was to follow them instantly. But, in this instance, my orders were not attended to. The boys had rushed upon Harvey and seized him. They were already violently discussing the question whether they should shoot or hang him for the crime he had committed. It was fortunate for him that my wrath, as well as that of Arnold and Painter, although fierce enough, was scarcely so savage as theirs was. Brighton Bill and Butch', I knew, would stand by me in almost any case, whether they agreed with me or not. If matters came to the worst, I also felt certain that we might count upon the assistance of George Laithrop. Rushing amongst them, it was with no small violence, and even a fierce blow or two, that I struggled to the side of the pale and weaponless Harvey, and wrenched him from their hands.

" What are you doing—Rangers ? "
" A' going to hang him, darned quick."
" Without even a trial ? " I demanded.
" We'll jist try him, arterwards."

"Then, by God!" I said, "you will have to hang me and try me afterwards, too." As they paused for perhaps half a minute, I continued without giving them a chance to speak. "I believed you chose me your Captain, yet here you are going to hang one of my boys, without letting me say a single word."

"Say it darned sharp, then, Cap!"

"And give us your orders to run him up with a rope, or put a bullet through his skull, in two minutes," roared out another.

As they were again crowding up and one of them had grasped Harvey by the collar, Ben Painter, followed by Arnold, had struggled to my side and thrust him back.

"I tell yer," he shouted out, for otherwise he would scarcely have been heard, "Mose is right. He's Captain. We mustn't have any Vigilance Committee business, but do up things square."

"We'll take him down to Susanville, and give him a fair trial," added Arnold.

"And then yer can hang him, if yer choose to," exclaimed Butch'. "Yer'll only have tu wait twenty-four hours."

By this time, the last speaker and Brighton Bill had vigorously thrust their way to my side, and I felt I had a sufficient support to carry my point and save Harvey from the menacing rope and tree which had so lately reared themselves before him.

But he also seemed to feel his increased chance of safety, and anxious to improve it, attempted to commence defending himself. When, however, he did so, I cut him short with a fierce whisper, announcing to him that if he uttered "a single word," I would abandon him. The Rangers were in a moment of such wild excitement, that, had he spoken, every effort we might have made would have been useless. Their savage fury would very speedily have settled the question, in spite of us. Even as it was, we had to contend with them for more than an hour, before we had calmed them down sufficiently to listen to our arguments.

When this was at last effected, I placed him in the charge of Painter and Brighton Bill, while we buried the man who had been slain through his insane want of judgment.

That night we slept in George Laithrop's house, and on the following morning we were no sooner stirring, than it was discovered that while we had been sleeping, Tom Harvey had been awake. In other words, he had made tracks.

It must be remembered that there was scarcely one of our party who, while engaged in active work, looking after the Indians, was not in the habit of keeping one eye at least half-open in the hours of his intermittent rest. Possibly, however, it was the belief that there was no actual danger immediately around us, as well as the security Tom's size and weight appeared to afford against any attempt on his part to escape, that prevented our slumbers from being broken. At all events, it was difficult for us to realize the fact that he had managed it. We were all of us sleeping upon the floor of the house. Our blankets were all we had. Beds were then a scarcity, in this portion of the West, as, indeed, they would be now, at any Ranch in a section of it not too thickly populated. How the deuce he managed to step over the prostrate forms of so many of us as were lying between him and the door, without disturbing one of the sleepers, it would be impossible to say. Had he made the error of half an inch, in placing one of his feet upon the ground, he could not have failed to waken the Ranger on whose body or limbs he must have trodden. Fear had evidently much lightened his person. In addition to this, I could not help suspecting that George Laithrop had connived at his escape. Of course, there was a frightful commotion about it amongst the boys, whose feelings of security amongst themselves had been so unpleasantly dispelled by his conduct. George, however, escaped without the slightest suspicion. If any one was imagined to have aided and abetted his flight it was myself and Harry Arnold. In fact, as we were riding back to Susanville, Butch' could not help saying:

"I'm darned if yer didn't manage the thing well, Mose."

After this, none of us again alluded to it. Life was too active and full of daily excitement, to give us time for recalling such an event after it had reckoned itself with the doings of the past.

Only once since then, did I hear anything of "Fatty." He had been seen by a trapper on the Humboldt River, and had then said he was on the way to Salt Lake City. He may possibly by this time have become a Mormon, and been enrolled as an elder of that polygamous community.

Some time in July, 1862, I received a letter from the last-named place. A few months earlier I had written to my wife, begging her to come to me, and giving her directions how to cross the Plains. This letter was from her. She had immediately complied with my wishes, and requested me to meet her as soon after she left

Salt Lake as might be possible. It would be impossible to express the delight which I felt in knowing she was so near me. None of those who have not experienced the pleasures of a life with little female society, and no near female relative to whom they can unbosom all their joy as well as all their weariness, discomfort, and trouble, can realize it. In the excess of my gratification, I fear I must have exposed myself to the laughter and jocularity as well as the envy of many of my comrades, as I cannot doubt but that, in my first moments of well-nigh delirious pleasure, I must have made a complete fool of myself.

Almost immediately, I left Susanville for Virginia City, Nevada. Thence, I went to Dayton.

Here I met an overland stage-driver. From him I heard that he had passed a train at Austin, in which I might find my wife. Accordingly, I purchased a horse and side-saddle from the keeper of the hotel, who was named Jaquish, and on the succeeding day was again in the saddle.

Dan Vanderhoof, a friend of mine whom I had known for several years, accompanied me portion of the way to Carson City. I went to this place with the view of meeting Colonel P. E. Connor with his command of California Volunteers. My friend introduced me to him and Major Gallagher, and I was asked to accompany them some eight miles down the Carson River to Reed's Station. It was to talk upon "business." Otherwise, I should have certainly declined deviating from the road, so increasingly anxious was I to see the little woman from whom I had so long been separated.

This business was, after the evening meal, speedily arranged.

They needed a guide and scout through Idaho and Utah, in the Fall. My qualifications as the last, would counterbalance any deficiency I might have as to the first-named. The necessary details were quickly agreed upon, and early on the next morning I was crossing the Desert towards the big bend of the Carson River. On the day following this, I came upon a large train of stock, and one of the guides told me a larger train was then some four miles behind them, at a distance of something more than a mile from the main track. Pushing on at once, in less than half an hour I came in sight of the encampment.

While I was riding up to it, my wife recognized me. How she was able to do so, has, on thinking the matter over, always astonished me. The tan of exposure on the frontier, fuller muscle, and the general style of my dress and equipment, had so thoroughly changed my personal appearance.

However, she certainly did know me. As for her, I should have recognized her features, even had she been dressed in the unsightly garb of an Esquimaux.

It would be little use for me to detail the words and actions of this meeting. Any man who has been so long separated from his wife as I had been, and any female who had, for so long a period, not seen the face of her husband, will readily imagine what passed between us. We were, nevertheless, quickly compelled to bring our outburst of natural joy to an end, by the approach of Chart Gregory with Mr. and Mrs. Devine, and others of her companions on the train. Then I heard of all the trouble she had been exposed to, and more especially of a fellow named Mat Carpenter, who had been consistently unkind to her since they had first struck the

Plains. He had been an old school-mate of hers, and had displayed the memory of their childish intimacy, by doing all he possibly could to increase the discomfort she had experienced in her preliminary taste of Western civilization.

"You needn't look round for him, Mr. P——," said Gregory, as he saw my eyes wandering round the camp, with an ominous look for him. "No sooner had your lady recognized you, than the scamp cleared out."

At the instant, the employment of my real name, for the first time in so many years, as well as the polite appellation he had bestowed on "Mrs. P——," so completely astonished me, that I momentarily lost my self-possession. After this I could not help laughing, as my wife also did, although she, very certainly, could not comprehend the motive which induced such an audible peal of merriment on my part. Then she told me that Mr. Gregory had already thrashed Mat, some two days since. At the same time he had told him, I should be made acquainted with his conduct the moment that I met the train. This very clearly accounted for his disappearance, without waiting for an introduction.

Having adjusted the side-saddle for my wife, and seen that she was safely mounted, I took behind me what positively needful articles she might require. With a friendly farewell upon our part, and a grateful leave-taking on mine to those of her fellow-travellers who had shown her kindness, we started across the great Desert.

Continuing all night, we broke fast next morning at one of the stage stations, and after resting for an hour, once more started.

From this point the road followed the river, and in my anxiety to save some eight or ten miles of a track which I knew must be toilsome in the extreme to a female whose life had not been passed in this part of the country, I cut across the low range of hills by an old Indian trail. When, however, I observed some Indians approaching from our right, I recognized the want of caution I had displayed. Without calling my wife's attention to their dark specks in the distance, for they were a long way from us, I urged the horses into a sharp gallop, trusting they might not have seen us. But the red man has eyes quite as keen as the white ranger. They changed their course, with the evident purpose of cutting us off from the river.

My decision was rapidly formed.

Knowing we should soon mount a small ridge, and should on its far side be unseen by them for some time, we had no sooner crossed it, than I turned left into the ravine known as Six-mile Cañon. Pushing rapidly up this, we made our escape, and I did not mention the narrow chance we had run of an Indian fight, until my wife and myself were in sight of Virginia City.

This was, I may undoubtedly say, the first case in which I had turned tail on the red-skins without an interchange of hostile salutations.

On arriving at Susanville, my friends told me that the Indians had, the day before, killed Loomis Kellogg and a man of the name of Block, beside wounding Theodore Perdum, at a place more than half-way between Laithrop's Ranch and Mud Springs. They had been attacked by a party of Indians, which were generally in the vicinity of Honey Lake and closely upon the Humboldt. These had been baptized by the settlers as the Smoke-creek tribe, although by no means a tribe in the same sense as the Pah-utes and Modocs were.

This band of red-skins was composed of the offscourings of these two tribes who had either fled or been chased from them, simply because they were too scoundrelly and contemptibly degraded, in the eyes of their original brethren, to be trusted or consorted with.

Smoke-creek Sam was their chief. He had earned this pre-eminence by being, at long odds, not only the most blood-thirsty villain in this gang of red devils, but perhaps the most irredeemable ruffian the Indian history of the West can chronicle. The outrages in which he and his band had been involved, both at our immediate expense and that of all the settlers anywhere in our vicinity, were well-nigh numberless. During the past year, whether Uncle Sam's patience had been worn out by the accounts he had received of his namesake's rascally and bloody offences, or from a wish to make some capital in the East by bestowing a little affection on his Western nephew, it would be impossible to say. He, however, condescended to bestow a little attention upon Smoke-creek Sam. Some blue-coats had been sent out, and two military posts had been formed. These were, respectively, on Smoke and Granite Creeks, in the centre of the sweep of country exposed to this scoundrel's depredations.

For a short time, he became somewhat quieter; but as the blue-coats did not busy themselves in punishing him, he had again plucked up courage, and since the Pah-ute troubles had anew commenced, was, once more, on the war-trail.

Harry Arnold had already called the Buckskin Rangers together, and they had determined upon starting for the purpose, if possible, of completely exterminating Smoke-creek Sam and his gang of cut-throats.

My presence in Susanville was speedily known by them, and I was unanimously called to take my position as the leader in this expedition.

The second honey-moon of my one marriage was, therefore, brought to an end, or, rather, indefinitely deferred. It had, most certainly, scarcely begun, unless the commencement of such an agreeable period of life may be supposed to take place in the saddle, and in flight from a party of hostile Indians.

Short time was allowed me to make my wife as comfortable as the exigencies of the moment permitted. The little woman submitted to them like a veritable heroine.

In something less than an hour, we were on our way to the spot where the murders had taken place. While going, we were joined by two companies of soldiers, ordered out for the same purpose. Captain Knight was in command of them; and shortly after we had passed Summit Lake, and reached the place where Fort Warner now stands, I touched on a fresh Indian trail.

My readers will not be unlikely to inquire how in the dry season of the year, when the cracked and parched earth takes no footprint, I was able to discern it. A small pebble here and there, freshly turned over, or a few stones formed into a sign for other red-skins, either to tell the day of the month on which they passed,* or

---

* These stones are ranged in a circle or semicircle, to indicate the quarter of the moon. Within these, the number of fragments of rock calendars the number of days from it. Other signs tell whether these indications are left by a war or hunting party, and how many of them there are. There are, besides, other marks, which tell whether the deer is in the velvet and all the changes it is subject to, which are invaluable to the hunter who is able to read them.

indicate the period of the year, are more than sufficient to the ordinary scout and trapper. In this case the first sign of a trail had been sufficient for me. It was clear that a very large number of the red-skins were in front of us, and, very certainly, scarcely as much as twelve hours ahead.

Consequently I sent Arnold up the side of the mountain, to see whether the red-skins might not be still in our neighborhood.

The Rangers were on foot, and I and Harry had been in advance of them. As I now continued, Captain Knight overtook me, almost immediately after I had been joined by Brighton Bill and most of the other boys.

"They say, Mose, you are on the trail?"

"So I am, Captain."

"I can see nothing!"

"Perhaps not. It needs quick eyes to follow this one."

"If there really is one," he said sharply.

His tone was not the most agreeably confiding possible, and I raised my eyes from the ground on which they had hitherto been fixed, to contemplate him, when Bill inquired:

"'Ow long, Cap, was it since the blamed cusses went by 'ere?"

"From four to six hours. Possibly, something more," was my answer.

The officer gave utterance to a low and very dubious whistle, which unmistakably suggested a disbelief in the authority Bill had appealed to. On hearing it the Ranger's bronzed face flushed, and he turned on the captain, exclaiming:

"What hin 'ell do you know habout hit? Hi'll bet my bottom dollar, Mose hain't made no mistake."

"Well, my lads," said Knight, who, I must do him justice, immediately saw the mistake he had made, "go ahead, if you feel so confoundedly sure of the rascals."

"In course we are," put in Butch'. "You just leave Mose alone, and we'll have their hair, afore night."

By this time, Arnold had rejoined us. He had as yet seen nothing. Leaving him, therefore, to follow the trail, I went up the mountain to try my luck. As I reached its summit, and cast a careless glance down the other side, which was bare of timber, I caught sight of what I believed must be our Indians. Some juniper trees concealed me. Descending a few paces on the side where I had left the boys, I swung my hat. They understood my meaning and came to a halt. Arnold and Painter very soon joined me, and carefully concealing our movements, we crept again to the summit. As they coincided with me, we immediately returned to our party.

Upon informing Captain Knight of what we had seen, he condescended to express his gratification, and immediately ordered his men to continue the trail we had hitherto been pursuing, and follow the red-skins round the far side of the mountain.

On my venturing to suggest that he had better send only a portion of his men up the valley, he inquired what reason induced me to advise such a division of his command.

"All the red devils are smart enough, Captain! Smoke-creek Sam is 'cuter than every Yankee pedler rolled into one, if that one had been between Honey Lake and the Humboldt for the last five years."

"Well! What if he is?"

"He's sure to smell us out. But if you will give me part of your men, I will take them with my boys across the mountain. Between us, not a red-skin shall escape."

"That's so, Captain!" said Harry Arnold, emphatically. "Mose gives good advice."

Whether or no Harry's opinion was so little flattering to his own judgment or not, that he was riled by the preference given to my counsel, modestly as it had been offered him, I am unable to say. With an obstinacy which may be a good thing in regular war, but is surely the reverse of it in following Indians, he would neither abandon his previous determination, nor give me one of his men. He, indeed, did all but order me to continue with him.

My back was now up. To his astonishment he found out that I was to the full as—perhaps, even more determined to have my own way in a matter I thoroughly understood, than he was. Possibly, although I do not like to venture such an opinion touching any of Uncle Sam's servants, he may have had no wish to catch the red-skins. In entertaining such a disinclination, he would only be imitating too closely the general policy of our respected relative.

Whatever his wish may have been, I ordered the boys to their saddles, and leaving him, struck a long cañon we had recently passed, which led us almost to the spot on which the Indians had just been sighted, whom Arnold and Ben Painter as well as myself believed to be the Smoke-creek gang. When we reached the valley in which they were, we found ourselves immediately ahead of the course they were taking.

No sooner had they spotted our party, which it was easy to do, in a tract of country almost entirely bare of foliage of any description, than they came to a halt.

We were yet far beyond rifle-range, and I actually thought they were going to give us the chance of a fair and square stand-up fight.

True, however, to their invariable character, the red men thought twice upon the matter. Turning from us they started up the valley, in the direction Knight's command was coming. However, they did not continue their retreat (it was a tolerably rapid one, as our pursuit also was) for more than a mile. Here they plunged into a rocky gorge on their left. Fancying that they might intend drawing the Rangers into a trap, I sent Brighton Bill and four others up the right side of the gorge, which was the most precipitous. Ben Painter, and some half-dozen more, were told to mount the other side. My directions were that they should advance as quickly as was possible, so that they might be able to head the party we were pursuing. It was fortunate that the ground presented tolerably rough travelling for horses, or, as they had necessarily dismounted, it would have been impossible for them to do this.

After pursuing the uneven and broken track in the centre of the gorge for a considerable length, perhaps some three-quarters of a mile, it turned suddenly to the right.

Here it formed a deep and irregular basin, from which there was only one means of escape.

This was a narrow and rocky defile, running up the steep side of the cañon. As they saw us behind them, they endeavored to mount this.

Bill, and the boys who were with him, had, however,

moved too quickly. Scarcely had they entered the defile, than he administered them a sharp warning to retreat.

Astounded by the totally unexpected warmth with which they had been saluted, they faced round, with the intention of fighting their way through their pursuers.

Upon reaching the bend of the gorge, at which it widened into this basin, Ben's party received them with a round volley.

The red-skins now knew they were fairly trapped, and drawing back into the basin, commenced, with the fragments of rock, to pile up a rude sort of breastwork. As the boys were dismounting for active business, a blue-coat suddenly appeared upon the scene. The soldiers had reached the mouth of the gorge, and Captain Knight had despatched him to find out what the firing he had heard, meant.

It must be owned, this was a sufficiently curious question. As Arnold not unnaturally asked the sergeant, who addressed it to me:

"What the devil could it mean?"

I replied even more sharply:

"You can see for yourself. If the Captain wishes to look at a little real Indian fighting, he's got a chance."

Time and words were, at this moment, too valuable for me to waste any more of them. I again turned to the work on hand, and the blue-coat rode back. It may be suspected he was glad enough to do so, as Indian bullets and arrows were at the time rather lively. We were left to finish the affair, without the slightest assistance from the paid servants of Uncle Sam. As we subsequently had reason to know, this was not, however, owing to any want of courage on the part of Captain Knight. His men had proved too cowardly to lend us a hand. They did not relish exposing themselves to the Indians. Neither the angry commands nor threatening appeals of their indignant officer could in any way induce them to give us an effective support.

Wrathful as we not unnaturally felt, we had no opportunity at the instant of discussing the matter with that righteous amount of Buncombe, which is, in similar cases, so gratifying to the average American mind.

It should be mentioned, nevertheless, that one of the boys became fearfully disgusted with the conduct of his paid protectors.

Indeed, Mart Gilbert, for such was his name, jumped from behind the mass of rock under which he was crouching. In his rage he actually executed an indignant *pas seul*, as I should in my earlier years have styled it, in the very face of the enemy. While displaying his maniacal agility, he roared out for any "darned red skunk" to show himself and fight him. None of those to whom he addressed himself, however, displayed any wish to accept his invitation. But, naturally enough, they thought they had an excellent chance afforded them for picking him off. A regular storm of bullets and arrows rang and whistled round him.

Fortune generally seems to have a sympathy with madness.

It certainly had so in this instance. Not one of these missiles even scraped his body. And before a second volley could be discharged at him, with, in all probability, a more successful result for the red-skins, Painter had crept to a point from which he could rake them a second time. This volley was delivered at short range and, as an officer of the regular army might say, destroyed their *morale*. As Ben subsequently thought proper to say, in a more vernacular phrase than I choose at present to employ, it impaired their digestion.

Seeing the disorder into which they were thrown, I gave the boys the order to advance.

My words were not quite rapid enough. The boys Brighton Bill had with him were once more in a position available for following the example those with Painter had set them.

Demoralized as they were by the second volley, the red-skins nevertheless exhibited what Saxons denominate pluck, and made a furious rush upon the main body of their assailants, meeting us about half-way up to their breastworks. Our work was now short and thorough.

Harry and myself had not dismounted. He was a capital horseman, and rode in Comanche style, better even than I did. It was in this fashion that he approached an old Indian who was literally hailing his arrows at us, and shot him from under the neck of his horse. Ridding his hand of the revolver which was attached to his wrist by a strap, he rushed the animal past his prostrate enemy, and took his scalp very neatly, almost at the same instant recovering his seat.

The red-skin, however, although dropped by Arnold's shot, very evidently disapproved of the loss of his hair. Raising himself from the ground, precisely at the moment when the former reappeared above the back of his horse, he let fly another arrow.

This struck Harry in the back of the neck, immediately behind the vertebral bones, passing directly through it for more than half its length.

No time was given the Indian for another shot, as I was sufficiently near to settle him.

"I say, Mose! lend me a hand."

On looking round, I could not forbear laughing. The manner in which the arrow had passed through Arnold's neck compelled him to protrude his head in front of him in such a strangely quaint fashion. Mirth would have been compulsory, even in one at the point of death.

Of course, while laughing, I had pulled out the unpleasant addition to his muscular anatomy.

Upon counting the bodies of the dead, we found seventeen. The remainder of the party had managed to effect an escape.

After this we returned to the mouth of the gorge, where we did not find Captain Knight and the bluecoats waiting for us. We felt considerably mortified by the fact, that although the slain red-skins might have been a portion of Smoke creek Sam's band, he himself was, as decidedly, not amongst them.

CHAPTER XIV.

ANOTHER ATTEMPT AT A HONEY-MOON—LEARNING AND LOVING—TWO UNEXPECTED RECRUITS—PLENTY OF WORK TO DO—A FEW OF THE SAINTS—WHAT A PITY HE IS NOT AN INDIAN—SIGHTING THE ENEMY—FREEZING WEATHER—SOME CLEVER GENERALSHIP—THE FIGHT IN THE RIVER—A NARROW ESCAPE—DESTROYING SUPPLIES—A LITTLE MINING—HOME AGAIN.

ON returning to Susanville, I had the satisfaction of resuming my interrupted honey-moon, and learning from my wife in our lovingly long talks together, much about my friends, which no letter is ever voluminous enough to tell. To say the truth, letters are nothing but the headings of the chapters of life, condensed according to the peculiar temperament of the writer. Sometimes, they give scarcely any idea of the real contents. Not infrequently, they afford an unqualifiedly false index to that which they are in a measure supposed to represent.

Moreover, she was far more of a woman than she had been. Self-dependence had in a measure changed her, as my life on the frontier had altered me.

I had to re-study her nature, as she very certainly had to re-learn mine.

There were many moments when, in spite of her love I caught her studying my face as if she was scarcely able to realize how completely the crude civilization of frontier-life had warped mine, for the better or the worse. While I, as frequently, detected myself wondering at the change a few years of absence had made in the girl I had loved well enough to tie myself to for life.

Yet, I believe, the change was not an unpleasant one to either of us. At least, I may safely affirm that it was not so to me.

The summer and great portion of the autumn passed but too quickly. Some few weeks of them had been spent with the boys at our mining claims on the Humboldt. Nor were we, on the whole, unsuccessful, having made a tolerably fair pile, in reward for our labor. When the autumn was nearly over, my companions went up the river as far as Gravelly Ford, with the intention of pitching their camp there for the winter. This was with the purpose of hunting and trapping. I had to keep the agreement already made with Colonel Connor. After leaving my pet bear, Charley, in the care of Butch', with whom he was almost as friendly as he was with me, I, therefore, again rejoined my wife for a brief time, while I commenced my preparations.

These were prolonged until the last moment, when I was astonished by a visit from Harry Arnold and Brighton Bill, whom I had left scarcely more than a week since at Gravelly Ford. In my surprise I asked:

"What, in the name of Heaven! brings you back here?"

"Can't you guess, Mose?" Harry asked.

"Has anything happened?"

"Nothing particular."

This was the reply of the previous speaker, as Bill added, with his peculiarly British pronunciation:

"We've made h'up hour minds to pull h'up stakes and join you."

"What do you really mean?"

The question was far from an unnatural one. My engagement with the Colonel had been repeatedly talked over with the boys when they were present. Neither of them, up to this time, had displayed the slightest indication of a desire to accompany me.

"To henlist with hour Cap!" exclaimed Bill.

"That's exactly what we mean."

I was but too glad to have them with me, and felt sure Connor would be even more pleased. A few hours were sufficient for them to get ready, and on the following morning the three of us quitted Susanville.

For some hours after leaving it, I felt as I had never before done, when starting on any expedition. The tear-blurred eyes of my wife kept painting themselves before me. It must be remembered how long we had been separated from each other, and how recently, for the second time, we had again commenced married life. Even the gay jests of Arnold, and the coarser, but equally well-meant consolation of Brighton Bill, failed to restore my usually blithe spirits until the noon was long past.

Movement and action, however, possess a large degree of comfort in them.

By this time I had recovered my equanimity, and on the following day I was as gay as either of them. Nothing of note beyond the common everyday occurrences of travel of this class occurred while we were on our road, until we reached Egan Cañon. Here we met some of Connor's men, who had been stationed there to protect the Overland stages. Thence we passed through Camp Floyd to Stockton, where we found the Colonel's command encamped near a small lake. Both he and Major Gallagher welcomed me in the most cordial manner. On presenting my two companions, whose names were well known to both of them, this cordiality was greatly increased.

"I knew we had secured one good man when we got you to join us," said Connor. "But I little thought you would bring us two more, as good as yourself."

He then informed us that we might take things as easily as we chose for the next few days, after which, he quietly said, he trusted to give us plenty of work. Arnold replied:

"The more of it, Colonel, the bettter."

The hearty readiness with which this answer was made, seemed to please him very much. When, shortly after, he left us, I heard him say to Gallagher:

"We are in luck, Major!"

Nor can I be charged with undue vanity, in supposing his congratulatory sentence referred to myself and my two companions.

We necessarily resigned ourselves to the comfort or discomfort, as man chooses to consider it, of doing nothing for the following week, or somewhat less. One morning, however, we were startled by a visit from the notorious Port Rockwell, Bill Hickman, Lot Smith, and others of the so-called Mormon Danites. Why they came was, of course, none of our business. Yet, we had heard too much of them to fail in examining them closely, and I am free to own I was not too deeply impressed by the sanctity of their appearance. The greater portion of them were, however, pretty muscular examples of saintship, and exhibited, what I always supposed they would, considerable oiliness as a veneer to their even less pure and peaceable proclivities. While we were inspecting them, I could not refrain from asking Arnold what he thought of them. He delayed a minute or two in making his reply, and Brighton Bill improved the occasion by propounding to me in a solemn, and exceedingly audible voice, the following query:

"H'i say, Mose! 'ave they h'all ha dozen wives h'apiece?"

"I suppose so, Bill," I replied with a quiet smile.

"'Eaven take care of 'em!" he ejaculated with a mournful air of pity.

"What? of these fellows?"

"No! Mose! H'of the poor lambs that hare tied hup to such ha blamed lot of Turks. H'if Hi had my will with the blackguards, Hi'd lock 'em hup, hin the Hold Bailey, or," he added reflectively, as if he feared I might not understand the character of the place he had alluded to, "four prison-walls for the 'ole of their life."

My companion had announced his views, with regard to the Danites, in tones which were something too loud. They were very evidently heard by Bill Hickman, who turned to look at him. As he did so, Harry for the first time spoke in a voice whose pitch was decidedly intended to reach the saintly ears.

"A truly delightful face, Mose!"

"Do you think so?"

"How I wish he was a red-skin!"

"Blamed hif you h'arn't right, Hank!" cried Bill, "'ow neat you could track and wipe 'im hout."

The part of this conversation which had been audible to Hickman, could scarcely have been highly agreeable.

Very certainly, I never saw a more diabolical scowl spread over any face, than did over his. It was, however, no very great length of time before they left us.

"I would scarcely advise you, Harry! to come in St. Hickman's way," I remarked when they were quitting the camp, "without having your revolver quite ready."

"I don't intend to, Mose!" he replied, with a sharp laugh.

Some two days after this, Colonel Connor detailed me to accompany a detachment under the command of Lieutenant Ether, up through the Bear River country. Arnold was assigned to another, which was to take the road through Ogden Cañon, while a third was provided with Brighton Bill as a guide, and were to go in the direction of Goose Creek and the City of Rocks. The two parties were to meet near Soda Springs.

Our detachment had only been out for a few days,* when I, who was a long way in advance, sighted a large body of Indians. Necessarily I fell back, and reported this to the officer in command. He immediately sent information of this to Colonel Connor. Afterwards, I heard that the two other parties had made a similar discovery, and sent him intelligence to the same effect. He immediately ordered his whole command to march towards Bear River, having sent instructions to the remaining detachments. The interval which elapsed before he joined us, was passed by me in keeping a keen look-out for the Indians. From the very first, I had seen that the colonel was a widely different class of officer from any of the servants of Uncle Sam I had yet met. If he meant business, it would be a pity to balk good intentions, and it should not be my fault if he failed to have plenty of it. Consequently, I did not

---

* During our absence, Colonel Connor established Camp Douglas, a few miles from Salt Lake City. It was on a rising ground, and very thoroughly commanded the Mormon capital.

feel disposed to let the red-skins slip, from my neglect to keep my eyes wide open.

No sooner had he joined us and received my daily reports from Lieutenant Ether, as well as the last one from myself, than he, in person, made a *reconnoissance*.

The result was, that he came to the conclusion already formed by me, that the Indians were concentrating their forces on Bear River.

It was in the dead of winter, and the temperature was intensely cold. The soldiers were suffering dreadfully, and but for the kindness and precaution of their colonel for them, many must have been lost or have perished by their exposure. He was a very strict disciplinarian. There was, however, not one of his men who did not love him the better for an inflexibility which was equally resolute in as far as possible providing for their comfort. This case was clearly one of necessity. If the Indians moved in this bitterly freezing weather, his men were obliged to move also. Nor did he shrink from sharing their sufferings and labors.

Consequently, on the following morning we started early on our way up the river, continuing until we were within ten miles of the Soda Springs.

Here, we saw the red-skins encamped in a strong position on the other side of the stream. It was almost a natural fortification, being protected by a deep cañon and huge rocks. While we were advancing, they fired on us. Their shots, however, failed. We were out of the range of their guns. Colonel Connor's dispositions for the attack were simple in the extreme, but very masterly. He ordered one party up the river to occupy a bluff which projected into it. Another was sent down the stream to take their position on the bank which commanded it, at no very great distance. The fire from either spot commanded the passage of the river.

When these two points were held, he ordered the main body to ford the stream, still keeping a portion of his force in reserve.

Bitterly cold as the water was, and as I found it, the soldiers did not evince the faintest shadow of hesitation when he gave the word.

Up to this moment, I believe the red-skins did not believe that Connor would attack them. Scarcely unreasonably, they counted too much upon their past experiences with Uncle Sam's blue-coats. In the present case, the blue-coats were tarred with a widely different brush. They had barely seen us in the river, than a rolling series of yells and whoops broke from them, which it would be utterly useless for words to attempt giving any idea of. The wall of icily chill water they had counted on to secure the front of their camp was useless. They had to fight, and dashed into the stream to drive back the enemy. Not more than one minute had they plunged into the freezing water, than from the bank and bluff rang out the rifles of the men Connor had posted there.

It was a terrible discharge, and drove them back. As they found themselves on dry earth, our gallant fellows followed them.

Dripping with the water, which would have frozen on them, but for the savagely fierce passion of that terribly mad struggle—shooting, clubbing, knifing, with the shouts and yells of actual devils—never do I believe a more bitter strife, considering its numbers, has been seen on any battle-field. It took two hours of hard fighting for us to completely rout them. This is the first time I have ever applied such a term to the defeat of a body of red-skins, simply because it is the first time in which I ever saw them really stand up and fight.

Often enough they slay when their numbers are fifteen to one, or are slain if the proportion chances to be an inferior one. It is, nevertheless, very rarely that they resist an open attack. This, more especially when it is made by any force which, in number, approaches their own.

When the last living Indian had fled, orders had been given us to destroy their supplies. There were several tons of dried meats, Government bacon, sugar, with no inconsiderable amount of whiskey and United States blankets, besides tobacco and other articles of native luxury. The red rascals had evidently a good commissariat, and had provided themselves for what they imagined would be a lengthy campaign. We also found a large quantity of powder. This we rolled into the river, and burned the rest.

In the meantime, our men who had not been employed in this necessary task, had been reckoning those who had been killed.

About one hundred and nineteen dead bodies were, I believe, counted in all.

The effects of the battle of Bear River were for the time decisive in pacifying this section of the country, and compelling the Indians in the whole neighborhood to remain quiet. And, may I not here, in all proper humility, ask our Government why it does not constantly employ such men as Colonel Connor to enforce peace upon the red-skins. Let it give us an Indian Bureau in the Cabinet. Place it in the control of such a man as General Sheridan, General Cook, or other almost equally able military men, whose names will readily suggest themselves to the reader. Give this Bureau unchecked authority to deal with the red man. It will sweep away the whole race of thieving Indian agents, and save the country many a dollar, as well as many a more valuable life which at present would seem to represent no positive value to the Government of the United States.

Perhaps, I should mention the narrow escape the officer, whose detachment I had been detailed to accompany on its advance in this direction, had, during the battle.

It was well nigh over. He was on the summit of a small ridge of rock which jutted from the eastern side of the camping-ground, when a red-skin fired on him, scarcely from a distance of some twenty yards. The ball missed Ether, but grazed the cheek of Hughey Greer, a private who was close to him. Wheeling round, Greer saw the Indian and took him between the eyes with a shot from his revolver, killing him instantly. Greer subsequently received promotion.

Naturally enough, the results of this victory enabled the Colonel to dispense with my services, although he would willingly have retained me longer with him. Shortly after, Arnold, Brighton Bill, and myself, therefore started for Idaho City, with the intention of again trying our luck in mining. We located a placer or claim on Bannock Bar, just above the Marion Moore claim. This turned out very favorably. After working it for nearly two months, we sold it to Henry Allen for a fairly round price, and determined upon making our return to Honey Lake.

CHAPTER XV.

OFF TO THE NEW MINES—"GOD'S COUNTRY"—A SHOWER OF SPARKS—THE CHEYENNE MAIDEN—SEEING IS BELIEVING— A SHARP WAIL—BEHIND THE BRUSH—THE LEAP LIKE A WILD-CAT—THE EFFECT OF UNPALATABLE NEWS—EVADING CROSS-QUESTIONING—THREE DAYS' FIGHTING—THE ENEMY PREPARING FOR VICTORY—ADVICE FROM EXPERIENCE—TWO BRAVE FELLOWS—BACON-FAT AND A KNIFE—WAITING AND HOPING.

BUT we were destined not to return as quietly as we had proposed doing. Upon our arrival at Boice City, we were induced to join a company who were going to Jordan Creek for the purpose of prospecting. It had been made up by Jeff Stanaford and another man of the name of Jennings. After depositing our gold-dust, therefore, with Wells, Fargo and Company, one of whose branch-offices was in this place, we started with our new acquaintances for the spot named, which Stanaford asserted from his own personal knowledge, was very rich. All told, our party numbered some twenty-seven men well armed and provided.

When some three or four days out, we camped at noon, about four o'clock, on a small rocky knoll, from the summit of which a deliciously clear and cool spring was oozing. Round the rise of this knoll there was excellent pasturage for our horses, and stretching beyond this on every side was a level plain, broken up with small sage-brush. At night-fall, our horses were brought in and picketed closed to the spring. No suspicion of the slightest danger was entertained by us. Indeed, we all of us slept soundly during the first part of the night, save Jennings, who was on the watch.

Some three hours before dawn, however, I became restless, and my slumbers were broken. A feeling of impending danger seemed to present itself to me, which I was unable to shake off.

Sitting up, I looked around. The night was as dark as pitch. Nothing could be seen by me, save the forms stretched upon the grass by the dying embers of the camp-fire, which scarcely gave light enough to detect them. I, however, managed to make out the figure of Jennings, who was sitting on the ground at a little distance. He was leaning forward upon his rifle, and was, I at once felt certain, fast asleep.

Possibly somewhat annoyed by this carelessness, I had caught up one of the half-extinguished brands from the fire, and was about hurling it at him, when I felt a light hand touch my shoulder.

The brand fell from my grasp as I rapidly turned, and the scattering sparks thrown from its burning end showed me a face which, since I had first looked on it, had never entirely passed from my memory.

How it was, my lips did not give utterance to a cry of astonishment, it is now, as it would have been then, impossible for me to say.

There were the superbly dark eyes, whose eloquence of expression I had never forgotten. There was that wealthy mass of raven hair, which had crowned the head of the Cheyenne maiden, for whom I had so nearly thrust from me the memory of the little woman I had left behind me in the East, or "God's country," as so many of the settlers and trappers call it.

It was Clo-ke-ta.

As she moved slowly away, I rose to my feet and followed her.

I seemed to be in a dream.

All I remember is, that the sleeper near me, on my right, stirred. My movement had startled him. He, nevertheless, did not wake.

Pausing for an instant where the horses were picketed, I once more heard her voice.

Although in a whisper, it was riper, fuller and more womanly than when it last sounded on my ears.

"Let my brother take his horse."

"Why should he do so? I asked in a tone no louder than hers had been.

"My brother must have many miles between himself and this place, before the dawn."

"And why?"

"Clo-ke-ta's master"—the intonation of this epithet was scornful, and, as it seemed to me, full of regret, which she disdained suppressing—"has his braves gathered around."

"Is Clo-ke-ta, then, married?"

I could not help the passionate inflexion with which I framed this whisper. For the moment, I had not only forgotten the wife who had so recently joined me, but the very information the Cheyenne woman had just given me.

"The daughter of Par-a-wau could not go childless to the grave."

"Certainly not," I answered mechanically.

My memory had bridged the intervening years between the present and the time when the parent of Clo-ke-ta, as well as Old Spotted Tail, had done me the honor of wishing to enroll me as a Cheyenne chief.

"Will my brother do as Clo-ke-ta has bidden him?"

The impatience of the request was more like her father's manner and voice than anything she had yet said. It recalled me to the life of my present.

"And who is Clo-ke-ta's husband?"

"A Bannock chief."

"The Indians from whom I am then to fly are the Bannocks?"

"My brother is right."

"Does not Clo-ke-ta know that the braves with her brother are numerous."

"The Bannocks who are waiting for the dawn, number more than the leaves of the sage-brush my brother has seen, before he laid himself down to rest."

Figurative as the expression was, there was no mistaking its significance. We were decidedly in for it, if her words were true, in even the thousandth or ten-thousandth part of her somewhat extensive style of reckoning the forces of our enemy. However, my experience of the Indian character for veracity had greatly modified the faith which, when I first knew her, I might have placed in her words. Considering our former relations, it would seem to be a matter of difficulty to make her understand this. But life in the hills and plains of the West considerably impairs sentimental delicacy in conversation, even with one whom a man had so narrowly escaped from wedding, as I had her. After a brief pause, I said:

"What the white man sees, he believes."

"What says my brother?"

"Let Clo-ke-ta prove her words, to his eyes!"

"The white chief does not think Clo-ke-ta has told him the truth!"

Her whisper was shapen so contemptuously that, at the moment, I could almost have bitten out my tongue in wrath at what it had given breath to. However, it was of importance that I should know whether her information had been exaggerated or not. I consequently replied :

"He does not."

Her fingers were laid upon my arm with an imperative gesture, as she whispered in a tone where scorn and affection were curiously blended:

"Let the white chief follow Clo-ke-ta. But his feet must be as light as the first leaf the autumn wind strews upon the plain."

As her last word fell upon my ear, she glided away from me. Nor was it without some difficulty I kept my sight upon her undulating form, as my steps sped noiselessly after.

We must have covered some eight hundred yards, or possibly less, when she pointed a little to my right, in advance of the spot we had reached. There I saw the struggling light of a small camp-fire, carefully smothered down with the torn-up roots of sage-brush, as I concluded, and could just make out the forms of the slumbering red-skins around it. Still further on the right I caught the faint glow of another. To the left, I could just make out two more; the farthest of these was so distant, that it was no larger, although less defined, than the flash of the fire-flies I had been accustomed to watch round my home in Galena, even earlier than the period at which I commenced this history of my adventures. As I turned towards her again, she said in a lower voice even than she had previously adopted:

"My brother has sharp eyes."

"He has."

"Does he now believe what Clo-ke-ta has told him?"

"Yes."

"And he will listen to her counsel?"

"He cannot."

"Why?"

"He is a white brave."

"Clo-ke-ta knows it."

"The red man might run away, by himself. Who would call him a coward?"

"His tribe would—"

She commenced thus, indignantly. Then she saw the error she was committing, and broke short off, as I continued:

"Without those who are with him can fly too, the white brave must remain."

A single sharp wail of grief rose from her lips. As it did so, I threw myself upon the ground and speedily commenced crawling back as rapidly as I could, to the camp.

Such a cry was enough to arouse every sleeping Bannock who might be within earshot of her, and quicken them to my presence.

One glance I cast upon her, before the darkness blotted her out from my sight. She was standing erect and motionless, and it appeared to me that she made a gesture with one of her arms as if to quicken my movements. There was no need for her to do so. The necessity for my reaching my friends was too obvious. Unless I was detected, she would be safe.

Already I had covered half the distance between the place, where I had paused with her, and our camp, when I rested for a moment. It was an almost compulsory

"'Does my brother now believe what Clo-ke-ta has told him?'"
—*Page 222.*

pause. The speed with which my retreat had been commenced, and the position in which it had been made, had for the moment taken away my breath. There was now also, in the darkness, no absolute necessity for my continuing my creeping posture. I had, therefore, half risen to my feet, when I caught the rapid sound of Indian footsteps. A red-skin was behind me.

Remaining upon my knee, I drew my knife, and listened. There was, evidently, only one who had disbelieved what Clo-ke-ta might have said. Possibly, although this is very unlikely, one only may have been awakened by her wail.

Had there been more than the one, I might have used my revolver, for the purpose of alarming the boys. If I had done so, it must have brought out the rest of the red devils. We had need of time for consultation. Could I get rid of my pursuer, without giving him the chance for one dying whoop, we should, at least, have this.

A clump of sage-brush would have hidden me from the rapidly approaching Indian, even had the dawn been already breaking.

He could only have fancied he heard my stealthy flight, as I knew I heard his rapidly approaching tread.

Now he was close to the sage-brush, behind which I was kneeling. An instant after, a dark figure, relieved against the comparatively lighter sky, is passing it. His limbs nearly touch me.

One leap, like that of a wild-cat, has fastened me upon him.

Fortunately my left hand has clutched him by the

throat. He struggles desperately, and attempts to shout. My knife was, however, ready.

In less than half a minute, all was over.

When I re-climbed the knoll, I found the boys already stirring. The wailing cry of Clo-ke-ta had aroused Arnold, who, finding me absent, had awakened the rest. Jennings could tell them nothing of my absence. Brighton Bill had proposed to Harry a search for me. The latter, however, saw that until the morning had broken, any such search must be worse than useless.

"And here are Mose, by Heaven!" ejaculated Jennings.

He rounded off his sentence with a fearful oath of delight, as by the light of the camp-fire, which had been heaped with fresh brush, he was the first to recognize me. Without a word, I was trampling out the flame, in which attempt I was assisted by Bill, who had a profound faith in my sagacity, and would, I firmly believe, have lent me a hand in cutting Harry Arnold's throat, had I thought proper to do so. When the affair had been accomplished, he would probably have inquired my reason for such a bloody proceeding, but not until then.

"What on airth! are yer about?" roared Stanaford. "Can't yer leave the fire alone?"

"Mose must have a sufficient reason," said Arnold. "Wait 'till he tells it to you."

"Hingins!" was Bill's suggestive explanation.

"Wall! arn't we enough for 'em?"

"Scarcely!" I answered. Then I added, as I trampled out the last burning embers with my heel, "they are all around us."

"How many?" inquired Arnold.

"I cannot tell, yet," was my reply, given with what, could it have been seen by him, was a grim smile. "Probably, some two hundred and fifty."

"Yer can't mean it!" exclaimed Jennings.

"Boys!" I then said, "we are in the tightest fix I have yet been in. They are Bannocks, and the Bannocks will fight, as you all know."

"How do you know what they are?" inquired Arnold.

A flush stole over my face as I delayed to answer. Had there been sufficient light to have detected it, I might have been exposed to an awkward cross-questioning. However, I replied:

"By taking one of their scalps."

This was a possible reason, although by no means a probable one, save in the case of an old Indian fighter. Nevertheless, it answered the purpose, for the announcement that we were, as it turned out afterwards, actually besieged by a large body of red warriors, was by no means adapted to raise the spirits of the men who were listening. Indeed, those of many of them dropped to zero.

Little more of the ordinary talk in a miner's camp was likely to pass between us, during the remainder of the night. It would not, however, be long for us to wait until the morning light verified my words. None of us cared about attempting again to sleep. We watched impatiently until the day broke. Then it was discovered that I had greatly under-estimated the number of the enemy. Although unable to reckon them, precisely, there were certainly more than five hundred redskins waiting to raise our hair.

When we realized our position, we saw that the contest against such odds must be almost a hopeless one. We consequently determined upon selling our lives as dearly as possible.

The first day passed in a succession of charges upon the knoll by the red rascals, broken by their repulse, and intervals of rest for us, following each separate attack. Our position was, by good luck, a remarkably strong one, and in these intervals we succeeded in greatly strengthening it. With our shovels and picks we tore up huge fragments of rock, with which we built ourselves breastworks, and excavated trenches for our own security, from which we could pick off the advancing Bannocks, whenever they indulged themselves in a charge.

At first, it somewhat puzzled me how Clo-ke-ta had learned of my being here. But my name, as well as those of Arnold and Brighton Bill, had become tolerably well-known among the Indians in the section of country around Susanville, and I at last concluded that it was known that all three of us were with the party. If so, the reason for these comparatively dilatory attacks was obvious. A prudent fear of exposing themselves to our unerring aim, kept them from resolutely putting an end to the matter.

During the whole of the ensuing night, a sharp lookout was kept up. None of our guards, who were regularly relieved at stated intervals, slept as Jennings had done on the preceding one.

Early on the following day, their Mahalas, or squaws, began to clear off a piece of ground beyond the range of our rifles. It was in vain, I attempted to recognize the form of Clo-ke-ta among them. Possibly she did not share their labors, although it is more than probable the distance prevented my sight from distinguishing her. While I was watching this operation, interesting not only to me but the rest of us, from its too evident intention, Brighton Bill said:

"Ha blamed pretty sight, hain't hit, Mose?"

"You know what it's for, then?" I could not help asking him.

"Hin course Hi do. H'it's ha kind hof theayter where the blamed Hingins mean to torture h'us."

"If they catch us, Bill!"

"They will have hus, sooner h'or later, that's sartain."

"They had me once, Bill. But while I have a knife, they shall never have me again."

"Hi'm blowed, Mose, hif you hare'nt right. Hi'll tell 'Ank, hand 'e and Hi will take care we're not roasted halive, too."

"You will be doing wisely."

After the Mahalas had picked the spot which had been selected as clear of sage-brush and rocks, as the back of a child's hand, they reared their rude and disgusting banners around it. Their design was perfectly clear. They intended to starve us out and take us prisoners. While we were discussing the probabilities of this, however, one of the Bannocks approached a little too near. It was a somewhat long shot, yet Arnold succeeded in dropping him. This excited the rest to fury, and they charged upon us with such a roar of whoops and yells, as seemed to be a perfect Pandemonium. Never have I, before or since, listened to such a devil's Babel. We shot two of them during the attack, which was repeated, again and again, during the remainder of the day. Its result occasionally varied. But on each attack they paid for it in something the same ratio.

On this afternoon they received reinforcements, and on the next morning their numbers again heavily increased. Arnold, indeed, calculated that there must, on the third morning, have been more than twelve hundred red-skins surrounding us.

Some discussion had on the second day taken place as to the feasibility of our cutting our way through them. This large increase in their force had, however, rendered such an attempt a matter of mere insanity. The whole of that day, they kept making dashes at us. Up to this, nevertheless, they had inflicted no damage upon our party. One result of their tactics, had, however, caused us serious uneasiness. Our ammunition was wasting gradually away. Moreover, our stock of provisions was running very low. It was clear, if things continued as they now were, we should not only find our guns useless, but might, if the Bannocks waited long enough, be unable to raise a finger in self-defence.

That night, it was evident to the most thick-headed amongst us, that it would be impossible for us to hold out much longer.

Things were looking desperate. We had already been placed upon short allowance for our stomachs. It had now become necessary to place some restriction upon our frequency of firing at the red devils. At the council in which we discussed our situation, two of us, named Gardiner and Jasper, volunteered to attempt passing the Indian lines during the night. If they were unable to procure us relief, they would at any rate perish in the attempt to do so.

It was a gallant offer. But they were like the rest of us, men of pluck. Had we not been so, necessity would have produced it. Nothing gives a man so much bra very, as the knowledge that his own courage alone keeps death at bay for a day or two longer. Their resolution was certainly increased by this knowledge.

Suffice it, this offer was accepted.

About eleven o'clock on that night, they stripped themselves perfectly naked, and, greasing their bodies with a portion of the bacon-fat which chanced to be left, prepared for their task. The reason for doing this last, was, in order to avoid their clothes catching on or being entangled by the brush, as well as to afford a chance of their escaping the grasp of the red devils, should their progress alarm them.

They were each armed with a sheath-knife. If caught, they had determined upon fighting as long as they had any life left to fight with. Neither of them would be taken captive. My experience, while in the hands of the Pah-utes, had been detailed to them on the preceding night, by Brighton Bill, in a full audience of the rest of our party. Nor did he narrate it, with mitigating circumstances. As may be very readily supposed, this had been by no means a highly consolatory recital.

It was, therefore, with a prayer for their safety from our lips, and with small hope of it in their own thoughts, that they left us.

The words in which our farewell had been uttered, seemed like bidding a last " good-bye" to actual brothers. Darkness had fallen heavily around us. We were unable to pierce the dense gloom with our eyes, and could see nothing. What was left to us but to wait and hope?

CHAPTER XVI.

A Good Shot—The White Horse—Approaching Help—Only a Flea-bite—A Shout of Joy—Raising the Siege—An Indian Panic—The Pursuit—Recovering my Senses—For the Last Time—A Bead and no Powder—Bare Feet and the Sharp "Shale"—Heroic Self-sacrifice—A Rapid and Dashing Rescue.

The hour of suspense which followed their having left the camp, was terrible. Every moment of it passed so slowly, that it appeared to be winged with lead. Each instant we were expecting to hear the crack of fire-arms, or the sound of a fierce struggle—not for life, but death. As the minutes passed slowly away, at length we began to realize the fact that they might have succeeded in passing undetected through the midst of the slumbering Indians. This belief gradually ripened into a positive certainty.

Brighton Bill was the first of us who found sufficient hardihood to give voice to this. Bringing down his hand with a ringing slap upon his thigh, he blurted out:

"May H'i be blamed, hif pluck don't pay hafter h'all. The boys hare safe."

"I'll bet they are," said Stanaford with a round oath. "The red skunks haven't nabbed 'em."

And so, that night, for the first time in three days, I was able to get some few hours of slumber, and woke with something akin to hope stirring in my bosom.

This day the Indians conducted themselves much as they had before done. We, however, were more prudent, and wasted no more ammunition save when we were sure of one of them. They, also, when they saw this, grew more cautious. Possibly, they were reasoning on our condition from the same stand-point we did ourselves. Seeing we wasted no more powder, they were probably reckoning that it was getting smaller in quantity, and thought it useless to run any more risk, until we were starved into making a dash for the open.

About the middle of the day, however, they began to tire of waiting.

A party of them would ride from their camp, and endeavor, by insulting gestures and exclamations of derision, to induce us to come out. This was always out of rifle-range. At length one of them, more daring than the rest, approached us within a hundred yards, and repeated their taunts. Stanaford, who was near me, said:

"I'll pick that red devil off, anyhow."

No sooner had he said this, than he dropped his cheek to his rifle, and in another moment the Bannock fell from his horse. Scarcely had he seen the Indian tumble, than, dropping his gun, he leapt out of the trench, in whose cover he was lying, singing out as he did so:

"I'll have his darned hair."

Jennings and the rest of us shouted for him to come back. This was of no use. He had reached the dead Indian and scalped him, before the other Bannocks realized what he was doing.

One of them, who was mounted on a beautiful white horse, and whom we had noticed on the preceding day, with a fancy that he must be some prominent chief, rushed towards Stanaford. Dropping on my knee, I was taking dead aim, when Jennings sang out:

"Hold on! Let me have a shot at him."

"Don't you be ha blamed fool!" roared out Brighton Bill. "Il'if the Cap don't 'it 'im, you can take my wig." Then he added, "D'idn't Hi say so?"

The last question was caused by the chief's falling backward and dropping to the ground, while his horse made straight for our camp. Like Stanaford, I was bound to take his scalp, and ran to get it. This was, nevertheless, close work. We had been right in imagining the fallen brave to be a chief. Almost as soon as he had dropped, and I was in clear view, some dozen or more of the red-skins made a rush for me.

Had they been a moment speedier, I should have exchanged my own hair for that I had taken.

The loss of their chief seemed to have excited them almost to madness. Every few minutes they would dash at us, shaking their clinched hands, brandishing their rifles, and yelling out taunts, which we were unable to comprehend, save from the beastly gestures with which they were accompanied. Their latter experience of our skill as marksmen, nevertheless, prevented them from getting within range of our guns.

The afternoon was rapidly passing away, when Arnold called my attention to some dust in the east. It was moving rapidly down the side of a small hill.

"White help!" he curtly said.

"Please Heaven! it may be, Hank!" I answered, as I watched the approaching cloud intently.

In a few moments, we were able to detect the forms of some fourteen horsemen coming straight toward us, at a rapid rate.

"They are a mere flea-bite for the red devils," he exclaimed, querulously. "However, we may make a better show, with them to help us."

The whole of our companions were now watching them, as also were the Indians, who commenced a movement, from our right and left, towards the approaching party.

"We must go to their assistance," I said to Harry.

"H'in course we must," cried Brighton Bill, making a step to the spot where our horses were.

"See!" cried Arnold, with a shout of irrepressible joy, "the red skunks are trapped."

When he uttered this, he pointed to one side of the knoll. At the same instant, Stanaford grasped my shoulder and called my attention to the other. Our attention had hitherto been so engrosed by the approach of this party, that we had not detected the advance upon either side, of two much larger bodies. These reckoned, as we subsequently learned, more than two hundred each. Gardner and Jasper had done their work well, and deserved all gratitude for the courage and speed with which they had carried through the work they had entered upon.

Moreover, the attention of the Bannocks had been engrossed with the approach of that party of our fellow-countrymen which I had, the very moment before, in company with Harry Arnold, noticed.

When they heard the rolling thunder of our shout of joy, and knew that we were mounting our horses, they gazed round upon either side. In an instant, they became aware of the manner in which they had been trapped. There was a moment of hurried consultation. After this, they seemed to be stricken with perfect dismay. The presence of our friends had smitten them with a thorough panic. A telling volley had been poured in upon their shrinking figures, when we charged upon them.

It was with the yell of a band of tigers.

Shouting, clubbing, striking, and stabbing, we broke in, upon all we came across.

For the time, we were in a complete delirium of savage rage. So much so, indeed, that no incident of the struggle can be in any way recalled by me, for the next two hours.

At the close of these, my recollection had come back. I was far to the north of our camping-ground. Noon was waning into evening. The blue sky of the morning was seamed and blurred with rushing cloud. The horse I was mounted on was urged by me, in a headlong chase, after two flying figures. In the commencing shadow of the evening, I was enabled to see that they were Indians.

Did I not recognize one of them?

What if I did do so? Was I not maddened with the long siege I had endured? Was I not wild from my lengthy imprisonment on the mound, and eager upon the work of death? Suddenly, one of their horses stumbled and fell. Its rider was thrown under the body of the fallen animal. With a wild scream of delight, I urged my own steed up to them.

When I did so, the other Indian had dismounted, and was standing between me and the fallen red-skin, in a queenly and defiant posture.

It was a Mahala.

"The white chief has killed the husband of Clo-ke-ta. Let him now, if he wills it, take the life of her father."

Par-a-wau was stretched upon the dry earth, crushed under the motionless body of the animal he had been riding.

For a moment, I gazed upon the two. My brain seemed to whirl in a wild dance, as I did this. Then it was stilled, and, without a word of reply, I leapt from the back of my horse. With some little difficulty I extracted the Cheyenne chief from beneath the dead body of the animal he had been mounted upon. The gallant little beast had been stricken, earlier, by one of our balls. It had passed through its hind quarter. Yet, in spite of the loss of blood and the weakness gradually growing on it from this, it had carried the Cheyenne thus far.

Although bruised severely by the fall, when I raised him, Par-a-wau was able to stand erect.

Neither of us spoke.

He, very evidently, supposed that it was my intention to make him a prisoner. In all probability, he had too much Indian pride to make any entreaty. Very possibly, he believed white blood might run in as hard veins as that of the red-skin. I led my own horse toward him.

"Will Par-a-wau mount the horse of his brother?"

Without a word of answer, he obeyed me. Then, I raised his rifle, which was still upon the ground, and placed it in his hands.

After this, I turned to the Mahala. She had been standing motionless, watching every movement which I had made. Touching her widowed brow with my parched lips, dry and smeared as they were with the grime of battle, I lifted her into the saddle of her pony, which had been standing near us, saying:

"Clo-ke-ta will sometimes think of the brother who has never forgotten her!"

As I quitted her side, I heard the same cry of anguish, which had been uttered by her, when I refused to obey her counsel and fly from the men with whom my lot was at the moment cast. My heart throbbed fiercely, yet I would not turn to her. Haply, she was thinking of the husband whom I had slain—perchance, she may momentarily have recalled the long-quelled dream of her youth. What was it to me what she was thinking of? Resolutely, I commenced my return.

In a few seconds after, I heard the tramp of the horse which had borne me, as well as that upon which I had placed Clo-ke-ta, ringing upon the plain behind me. Par-a-wan had breathed a few words to his daughter, as she passed from my hearing, in their own tongue. It almost seemed to me, as though a portion of my life had been torn from me.

Treading rapidly along the plain, I was buried in the mingled gloom of the present and the past.

Yes! This was the end. My hand had widowed the woman, for whom I had once been so sorely tempted to forswear civilization.

In spite of the excitement of the last few hours, my thoughts were for the moment with the past, when they were suddenly brought back by a voice, whose tones I had recently become more than well acquainted with. They were characterized by a somewhat coarse and insolent surprise.

"Wall! I swar, if this don't beat all. It's Buckskin Mose."

This exclamation was followed by the heartier and more energetic utterance of Brighton Bill.

"Hi'm blamed, Cap, hif you weren't lucky; we 'adn't no more powder."

"Whar's yer horse?"

"May Hi be blamed hif h'it hain't nabbed by them

thieving Higgins. Nare' a matter, Mose; 'ang me hif Hi don't get h'it back for you."

Bill's horse was already plunging by me, when my grasp was on its bridle.

"You won't, Bill!"

"What d' you mean?"

"What I say!"

Jennings, the man who had been with Bill when the two had caught sight of me, was already some ten yards from the place where I was standing.

"Come back!"

Glancing over his shoulder at me, he saw me drawing a bead upon him. Not knowing I also was out of powder as well as himself, he thought it best to pull in and return, swearing at what he considered my stupidity. The opinion of Brighton Bill was, however, of greater importance in my estimation. This, the more especially, when I found out he evidently had settled my conduct as an undoubted example of temporary insanity. At any rate, I saw him, when he fancied my glance was turned away, looking at Jennings, and touching his forehead in a very significant manner.

"What are you thinking of, Bill?" I asked him, suddenly.

"Nothing, Cap! Hi'll be blamed hif Hi am. H'only hit's queer."

And so, I can scarcely doubt, it seemed to him. Returning to the camp on foot, I neither explained in what way I had lost my horse—whether it had been shot, stolen, or run away. Nor did I in any way allude to my share in the battle. My questions were, however, numerous enough during our return. The Bannocks had, indeed, been completely routed. Saving Colonel

Connor's defeat of the Indians on Bear River, it was the most terrible defeat the red-skins had met with, since I had taken up my residence in this portion of the country. As I afterwards learned, some four hundred of them had been slain, and almost as large a number of horses had been captured.

By the bye, I may mention that the white animal previously mentioned, subsequently was known as one of the fleetest race-horses in all Idaho.

On our way back to Boice City, the party who had come to our rescue related to us the adventures and sufferings of the two brave fellows who had succeeded in carrying them intelligence of our position.

After quitting the knoll upon which we were besieged they had commenced their stealthy advance through the Indian lines, crawling flatly upon the earth, like a serpent. Each of them had taken a different direction. Frequently they passed close to a slumbering Indian. But for the grave necessity which imposed every precaution upon him to avoid detection, Gardner said more than once, he was tempted to knife some of the red devils, who had reduced him and the rest of us to so sore a strait. However, feeling that if he did so the struggle he might possibly cause would rouse the camp, he had wisely enough refrained from doing so.

After they had passed their enemies and were some mile or more beyond them, each rose to his feet.

Jasper had followed a small creek for some distance, and then struck across the rock and shale of the mountains until he reached Boice City. His body was scratched and cut by the brush he had stricken against in the commencement of the route, while the flesh had been actually torn from his feet by the jagged shale he had passed over. When he arrived in the city, those who first saw him fancied he had just made his escape from the Indians, who had been amusing themselves by torturing him. Gardner had struck in a more northerly direction for Idaho City. His way had been nearly as bad, and he was almost dead when he arrived there. It should be mentioned that the former of these two unrecorded heroes died within a short time, after reaching Boice City. He had, voluntarily, as Gardner had also done, exposed himself to the almost sure risk of death, on behalf of his companions. Peace be with the gallant fellow, in that long sleep, for which we shed tears of blood!

No sooner had his information been given than Jake Jordan leapt upon his horse, and stopping at every house, called for volunteers. Every horse was placed in requisition. They were even taken from the teams that were standing in the main street, and mounted by those who were eager to join the expedition, whether their owners or not.

A well-equipped party soon after came in from Idaho City, and joined them.

When everything was in readiness, and not a moment had been lost by them, they placed themselves under the command of Jordan, and took the road. Nor did they slacken rein, even for an instant, until they had so bravely opened the doors of the trap into which we had unfortunately fallen. It was one of the most rapid and dashing rescues I ever remember in the West, and does infinite credit to him who carried it through, in every particular, with such complete success.

CHAPTER XVII.

The Respectable Pile and an Idle Winter—Only One Street—Gambling and Drinking—A Western Communist—"Keerds"—A Sticky Wrist—Eight Hundred per Cent—North or South—A Blow for the Old Flag—Neck or Nothing—A Compulsory Cold Bath—Not very much Damaged—Unable to get Compensation.

After a somewhat brief rest, Harry Arnold, with Bill and myself, determined upon returning to Honey Lake Valley. Nothing worthy of notice occurred until we reached Susanville, except that we travelled by night, and lay in camp during the day, to avoid the chance of discovery by any scouting party of Indians.

It was now late in the year, and as, after hearing the danger I had run, my wife was unwilling that I should so soon leave her again, we determined, with the balance of the Rangers whom we had left on the Humboldt, to pass this winter in comparative rest. That is to say, we would hunt deer for the market in Virginia City, and set a few traps.

The probability is that we arrived at this conclusion, from the fact that we had all of us more or less made money during the past year. Those of us who had been mining nearer home had done sufficiently well; while, in addition to what the three of us had been paid as guides by Colonel Connor, we had gathered a very reasonable pile of gold-dust while in the neighborhood of Idaho. Consequently, we were all of us disposed to enjoy the proceeds of our toil, and do as little hard work as possible.

My first business was, of course, to see to the comfort of the little woman whom I had been again absent from, for so many months.

Indeed, there was some surprise on the part of my friends to find me now and then declining, not only to join their hunting expeditions, but in addition sometimes refusing to form one in their raids upon the Faro and Monte banks which were run in various saloons, one of the most notorious being that in Burkett's Saloon, kept going by Heap and Hale, the John Chamberlains of Susanville. It will, probably, not astonish my readers to hear that these raids were by no means altogether flattering in their results to the skill and good fortune of the Rangers.

There is one anecdote which will not prove unamusing. It is, indeed, so characteristic of the inner life of the place, as well as of the general inner life of the mining districts, that I cannot refrain from recounting it.

Up to the present time, I have neglected to describe Susanville. It was by no means a large city, according to the Eastern notion of what a city should be. Nor, possibly, did it enjoy an over and above large share of civilized respectability.

A single street contained the whole of its actual business population. And of what was this whole visible street composed? Almost entirely of frame buildings for the retail of ardent spirits; in other words, of drinking-saloons. "Good Old Bourbon," "The Best Cognac," "Capital Rye," and other inviting appellations, of the same class, were the only evident appeals to those who chanced to pass through it, for their custom. Occasionally, indeed, you might find a liquor-store which in a measure protected a different class of business. In the front of one, you might find piles of ready-made clothing. Within another were all the appliances for three-card Monte or Faro. Here, were cigars and tobacco. This one, also, did duty as a corner-grocery.

These places were generally left to their own care, from the hour at which they were closed until the following morning.

The honesty of frontier-life protected them from being broken into.

At this time there was living in Susanville an aged settler named Pascal Taylor, but more commonly known as "Old Zac." He was an independent sort of Communist. Did he need chicken for a pot-pie, he would appropriate the fowls of his fellow-settlers without the slightest scruple. If he needed a new pair of pantaloons, it was equally indifferent to him whether he made a requisition upon the piles of clothes in front of the store of a dealer of such articles, or upon the dwellings of his nearest neighbors. However, let me do him justice. When detected, he would invariably repay the injured party in kind, by appropriating another article of the same sort and bringing it to him.

In fact, he might be termed a continual debtor to life, paying, from time to time, by incurring another debt. Whether at the close of his career his account with life might be balanced, must, nevertheless, remain a matter of considerable doubt.

Tom Long was the owner of one of the drinking-saloons, I have mentioned, as composing the line of street or road which was named Susanville. His residence was on the hill rising from one side of the line of liquor-shanties in which its regular inhabitants made money. One night, old "Zac" was standing beside the spot where Tom was dispensing liquor. He was a favorite of Tom's. For what reason he was so, it would be impossible to say. But Tom employed him to do up odd "chores" for him, and occasionally assisted him in a way which in the East might have been stigmatized as "red-hot" charity. In Susanville, it was not considered so. Old "Zac" was a privileged person. Well, the truth is, Tom was tired with the employment of the day. He wanted to quit business and retire to his home. Turning to "Zac," he pushed out the bottle and a tumbler.

"Take a drink, Zac?"

"You bet—" responded the recipient of Tom's bounty. "I say," he continued, lifting the Old Rye to his lips, "here's long life to you."

"I want to go home."

"Why in thunder don't yu go, then?"

"Zac, I think I will, if you'll 'tend business for me."

"You bet!"

"Thank you, Zac! Here's the key of the door. Mind you lock it in about half an hour, and open it again, to-morrow morning." As Tom concluded, he took a fair dose of Rye himself, to render his skin impervious to the night air. In this he was imitated by old Zac. Then putting on his coat, and taking his hat, he quitted the saloon with a cheery "Good-night, old boy!"

Now, "Zac" had no intention of remaining long after his friend and patron had gone. He had rinsed out the two glasses he and Tom had just emptied, and was on his way to the door, when four of us stepped in.

"Eh, Zac! whar's Tom?"

"Gon to hum."

"Wall, you'll du!" exclaimed Butch'. "Jest, shet the doors."

"Hi'll see to hit better than 'e will, by ha blamed sight!" said Brighton Bill.

At the moment he said this, he was striding to the back-door of the saloon, which he very coolly locked and put the huge key in one of his pockets. No sooner was this done, than, returning to the front entrance, he performed the same operation.

Butch' had meanwhile seated himself at a square deal table in one of the corners of the room.

"Whar are the keerds?"

"Here—you bet!"

Ben Painter produced the pack, and was speedily, with myself and Bill, seated at the other three sides of the table. Our gold was produced, and laid beside us. At that time, as now, paper money was an unknown quantity in California. Then we began to play.

During the whole afternoon, we had been drinking. Necessarily, after playing for some fifteen minutes, we felt somewhat dry. Butch' possibly felt drier than any of us. At any rate, he was the one who cried out:

"Bring up the licker, Zac!"

The old fellow brought us the Rye and four glasses on a tray. We drank. But when he had again removed the glasses and held out his hand for the four "bits," or twenty-five-cent pieces, habit required, his unprincipled customer produced a revolver which he very deliberately cocked and laid down upon the table beside him.

"D'yu see that?"

"You bet—Mr. Hasbrouck."

"Wall, then! don't stick out yure paws for money but bring along the licker when we ask for it."

Old "Zac's" lower jaw dropped as he looked in the face of him who spoke. There was a general shout or rather scream of laughter from the three other card-players. The face of Butch' was, however, as inflexible as if it had been hewn from granite.

"What du yu mean?" was the question at length propounded.

"Exsag'ly what I say. Jest mind your business, and we'll mind ourn."

After this, we continued playing.

California had, before this time, a monopoly of such rough and possibly dishonest jests. The very men who would have scorned implicating themselves in any business swindle, saw no harm, in occasionally, when under the influence of liquor, perpetrating a joke of this description. When younger, Taylor himself may have been an accomplice in some of the same sort. He walked back to the bar, with a countenance as grave as that of a man who is going to the gallows.

Speedily another round of drinks was ordered. This was followed by another and another.

Occasionally I glanced at him, and saw the hard lines of his countenance growing longer and longer. At last, about one o'clock, when we had been playing for some three hours and the log on the hearth had burnt down to scarcely more than a white mass of wood, which would have blistered any hand that touched it even while it threw out no heat, we felt the place growing cold. Old "Zac's" face lost its melancholy at the moment when Ben Painter sang out, with a lusty shiver:

"Put another log on the fire, Zac!"

"Whar am I to git one?"

"What d' yer mean?"

"You bet, Mr. Painter! I hain't got the key. How in thunder am I to go fur wood?"

The old fellow was quite right. How in thunder could he go to the wood-pile, while the door was locked? It was dangerous to let him have the key. He might run to Tom Long's, and inform him of our use of the contents of his cellar, without cashing up. Tom Long was by no means such a pacifically disposed individual as his temporary substitute. A similar thought to this evidently suggested itself to the mind of Brighton Bill. Rising from his seat, he said:

"Hi'll go with 'im, and may Hi be blamed hif the hold rip bolts."

Some time elapsed before the fresh log made its appearance, and the door which Bill had opened was once more locked. The log was placed upon the embers by old "Zac," and, in a brief time, the cheerful blaze from it was again warming the chilly temperature of the saloon.

We recommenced playing. Presently more drinks were called for.

As before, the old fellow brought them. This time, however, he had not placed the glasses upon a tray. He brought them two in each hand. Leaning across the table he placed the first two between Butch' and me. The other two were planted between Painter and Brighton Bill. As I chanced to look at him, shortly after, I saw the roughly rigid lines of his mouth actually curving into a smile. When another round of drinks were demanded, they were brought in the same fashion, but placed between Brighton Bill and Butch', and between Painter and myself.

Shortly after this, it struck me that my pile of eagles had lessened more than it should have done.

I and Bill had, however, been losing. The probability was that I had not noticed how rapidly my money was going. Nevertheless, when drinks were again called for I saw old "Zac's" wrists on Butch's money and Painter's, as the two glasses were set down, between them and the remaining two players. When Long's substitute left the table, it was clear fewer gold pieces laid between them and us than had been heaped there before. I was on the trail and followed it with my eyes. When I had detected, however, the means of which the shrewd old vagabond had availed himself to get even with us, I was too much amused to turn State's evidence, even in the row which ultimately arose between Brighton Bill and Butch', from the former accusing the latter of concealing his winnings. Bill had lost about as much as I had. He was, nevertheless, unaware that his crony, for such next to myself Butch' Hasbrouck was, had lost equally in amount, although more in proportion, than he had himself.

The astute "Zac" Taylor had managed to prolong his apparently enforced embassy to the wood-pile, until he had been able to cover the lower sides of his wrists with pitch.

This shrewd dodge had enabled him to pay Tom Long or himself, seven or eight times more than the amount due the former for the liquor we had been consuming. Every time he stretched across the table to place two glasses upon it, or repeated the action by my side, his wrists would rest upon two of our piles of gold pieces.

Each time, one or two half-eagles were secured by the pitch with which the old scamp had anointed the side of his wrists necessary for this shrewd trick. The consequence was, that, for the only time in my life when such an unusual chance occurred, the whole of the four players were almost dead-broke.

But for the quantity of rye we had all of us been swallowing, the others must have seen through this impudent operation as I had done.

If so, it may be a matter of question whether "Zac's" undeniable popularity would have saved him from an entire coating of the pitch he had so acutely employed. Relishing the trick, I, however, held my peace. Possibly, had it occurred when flush times had passed, or before they had begun with me, I might have acted differently.

Early in the next spring, as our funds had almost touched low-water-mark, the boys held a council of war, and it was decided upon, without a single dissenting voice, that we should once more try our luck upon the Humboldt River.

Accordingly we started to the mines, there. For the first time we met in this locality with indifferent success, or rather with no success at all. We, therefore, decided upon prospecting at a further distance, and repaired to Austin. Here we found the mines less promising even than those we had just left, and pushed on to Belmont in the hope of doing better. A similar want of fortune pursued us to this place.

One evening as we were sitting in camp, in no very agreeable mood, as respected the world and things in general, a bright idea struck one of us.

"Look here, boys!" he said. "Haven't you ever thought of fighting ag'in Secesh?"

"Each time one or two half-eagles were secured by the pitch with which the old scamp had anointed the sides of his wrists necessary for this shrewd trick."— *Page* 248.

"May Ili be blamed," exclaimed Brighton Bill, "hif you 'aven't 'it hit! What's the h'use of prospecting hand digging where we don't git nothing. Hi'm game for heither side. Let's go h'in, Cap!"

"I'm not exactly game for either side, Bill!" was my reply; "but for the old Stars and Stripes, I think I'd like to take a turn."

"So would I. It will be some variety, old fellow, in any case, 'though I'd as soon fight it out on either side," said Painter.

"So would I. Ye're right, Ben!" ejaculated Butch' Hasbrouck.

"We'll put it to the vote, which side we go in for, Mose," quietly said Arnold.

Not one of us declined fighting. It was merely a question as to which side the fight was to be entered upon. A brief discussion had the result of our taking Harry's advice. The old flag, however, carried the largest number of votes. We were to strike a blow for the Union.

After we had determined upon this, the next thing which presented itself to our consideration, was the line of travel it would be best for us to take. We had a fair stock of coffee, sugar and jerked meat. This would, however, be insufficient, if we intended to cross the continent. We should have, consequently, to direct our march through a section in which game would be tolerably plentiful. My suggestion was that we should pass through the Paranagut country and the southern part of Utah, until we struck the Colorado River. From that point our line of march would be clear enough.

"Have yer ever been through that part, Mose?" asked Butch'.

"No."

"Then yer've a darned good nose for game, I will say."

"And red-skins, too," said Arnold, "if we are to believe all we hear."

"Whar thar's game, ye're sure to find the skunks," exclaimed Painter sententiously.

And so, the first part of our route was settled without much difficulty.

Next morning we broke up camp, and after a few days of hard travelling, struck the south fork of the Colorado. Game had been scarcer than we had supposed. However, it was absolutely necessary that we should here replenish our stock of provisions. The jerked meat began to run low, and we had no more than a single day's rations of coffee on hand. A halt for a few days was therefore proposed, during which we might devote our time to hunting, and laying in sufficient meat for us to continue our route to the East.

On the second morning after we had camped, I started alone up the river.

After ascending it for some three or four miles, I crossed and broke from it towards the south. In a brief space of time, I spotted an antelope, and was creeping up to it, against the wind, when almost close to me, beneath a large rock which had hitherto concealed it, I caught sight of another. My rifle was in a moment at my shoulder, and with no more trouble than it takes in telling it, I rolled him over.

This had occurred in the afternoon, and as I should have to carry the animal back with me, I thought it might be as well to retrace my steps.

Tying its feet together, I accordingly slung the dead antelope upon my back and started on my return.

The side of the Colorado in which our camp had been pitched, swept down to its banks with a park-like slope, although its herbage and the trees with which it was broken up, were wilder and more luxuriant than such a qualifying epithet might lead the reader to suppose they were. On the side to which I had crossed, the stream was bounded by an almost perpendicular wall of cliff, about sixty or seventy feet in height. Calculating that I should readily find some spot at which to descend, I had taken my way almost in a bee-line to the spot opposite our camping-ground. Scarcely had I covered more than a mile in this direction than, happening to turn my head to the left, I saw a number of red-skins rushing towards me.

So thoroughly unmolested had our party been by Indians, since we had left Belmont, that I had entirely forgotten Arnold's warning hint about their presence in this part of the country. Indeed, I had not even thought about them lately, so apparently secure from their presence did we seem to be.

Here, however, they were, and plenty of them. Dropping the antelope in order to save myself, I took to my heels.

On arriving at the top of the cliff, immediately opposite the camp, I found no place at which I could manage to reach the bottom. The side of the cliff appeared to be one unbroken wall of rock.

Dashing up the river along the summit, at a little distance above I found a small notch in its face, haply, worn by some one of the numerous rivulets which seam the hills and mountains in winter. This afforded a means of partially sliding down or dropping to the level of the stream. The boys, on the opposite side of the

Colorado, discerned me just as I had discovered this. They also saw the Indians, who were gradually closing upon me, and a volley of balls rattled amongst them.

At the same time, I had dropped upon my knee behind a rock, and given one of them a very conclusive hint, that, on his part, at least, any further pursuit of me must be useless.

But my discharge had scarcely rung upon the ear, than two red-skins had seized me.

They had attempted to cut me off, and my unlucky wish to take a hand in the play of my friends, had given them the chance of succeeding. In the struggle my rifle was kicked over the brink of the precipice, and fell into the river. I had dashed one of the Indians from me, and had gripped the other by the throat, when they were joined by two more. Forcing me upon the ground, they speedily tied my hands together, and dragging me from behind the rock to the brow of the cliff, in plain sight of the boys, threw me over.

The next thing I remember was the voice of Brighton Bill.

"H'it's ha blamed good chance," he said to some one who was standing by him, "'e didn't smash 'is 'ead hon the rocks, or 'e'd this time be ha goner. H'i guess 'e'll go 'ome now, hand give hup wanting to fight for Huncle Sam."

"He'd do the old boy more good by ridding the country of them cussed red devils, than by any other way," was the reply of Butch'.

Bill had seen my body flying over the face of the precipice. He was an excellent swimmer, and, almost as I struck the water, had plunged in after me. When I heard what Hasbrouck said, I endeavored to speak, but for some moments could not manage to make a single word audible; while the boys, seeing the motion of my lips, were crowding round me, and uttering every class of kind comfort, and not unchristianly profane tenderness. When, at length, I was able to find utterance, it was to Hasbrouck I spoke.

"You are about right, Butch'. We'll first wipe out some of these cursed Apaches."

"How do you feel now, Mose?" asked Arnold, upon whose knee I found my head was resting.

"Not very much damaged," I replied, as I managed to sit up, "except by the loss of my rifle."

"Hif that's hall," said Bill joyously, "Hi'm blowed hif you're much 'urt. H'as for your gun, Painter can tell you h'if hit's much hout hof geer."

"It only got a good wetting," was Ben's answer. "It war wuss for the cartridges than 't war for the barrel."

Like a practical man, he had been employed in taking it to pieces, drying and cleaning it, after Bill had dived for it and brought it to land with him.

"Now, tell us, how you got into this darned scrape, old boy?"

In compliance with Arnold's request, I gave them a thorough narration, and as the moon had risen and it evidently promised to be a clear night, in another hour some half of the Rangers crossed the Colorado to look after the antelope, and if they could to pick off one or two of my assailants. However, they succeeded in finding neither antelope nor Apaches. The last had carried off not only all of their own scalps, but also the carcass of the game I had counted on for our supper.

We remained in this part of the country for some little time.

Nevertheless, we scared up no more red-skins. The Apaches, perhaps, had more respect for our rifles than the Bannocks lately had. Possibly, also, they were, at the time, not in force between Prescott and the Colorado. In any case, we saw nothing of them, and were unable to punish them for their disturbance of our hunting. In addition to this, we killed very little game, and at length crossed from Prescott down the Gila River to Fort Yuma. Thence, after remaining in its neighborhood for a few days, we returned and followed up the Colorado, through the Mojava and Navajos settlements, occupied by partially civilized red-skins, until, late in September, we once more found ourselves in the Honey Lake Valley.

CHAPTER XVIII.

CIVILIZED LIFE IN A LARGE AND YOUNG CITY—WHAT A RED-SKIN WOULD THINK OF IT—A CHANDELIER AND A BONFIRE—THE OLD FRIEND—THE WELL-KNOWN PIPE—TOO OLD TO KILL—SPITTED—THE WHITE MAHALA—AGAIN IN CO-OPERATION WITH THE GOVERNMENT—THREE MORE INDIAN MURDERS—OUR INDIAN RECRUIT—"SHOOT HEAP, BUT NO GUN"—"A CONVARTED RED DEVIL."

THE following winter was passed by me in San Francisco. It was for the first time since I had joined Captain Crim in crossing the Plains, that I had trodden the streets of a large city. All seemed to me so new, so busy, so thickly populated, that, for a few days, it appeared to me like the real Wilderness, while I looked back on the mountains, the forests, the cañons, and the desert I had left, as my actual world.

My feelings partially realized those of the savage, when for the first time he treads in the active marts of trade, and their equally laborious wealth or poverty.

Mingling with his wonder at the thronged and toiling stores, the superficial wealth everywhere apparent, the spars and masts of the huge shipping, the numerous spires, the sloping-eyed and high cheek-boned Chinese, the buzz of countless life surging around him, the clanging bells from the churches, haply the decorated volunteers stepping out to the voice of drum and trumpet, with the elegantly dressed women, the inanely simpering dandies, and blear-eyed spectacled old men, who have been working on and on without pause or cessation for scores of years—there cannot but rise in him a feeling of contempt for all he sees before him.

He may not but contrast his own chainless and unfettered existence with that walled-in life whose passions are merely, so it would appear to him, things of routine; whose enjoyments seem to him meaningless shadows; whose loves and hates would count in his eye as nothing; and whose range, from the cradle to the grave, is to him narrower than the glad gallop of a single day on which he sights his game, or spots his enemy.

But what have I to do with such thoughts as these? My white friend cannot realize them—nor can my red enemy even read them. The first will consequently laugh at me for indulging in, while the last will never hear of my having entertained, any such reflections.

Moreover, after the first week of my sojourn in San Francisco, they gradually wore away. In my early life, which had been for so many years almost forgotten, I had been upon the stage, had dealt in pop-corn, and had proven my skill as a detective. If I could now find no occasion to employ one of the last-named class, I could in any case purchase and eat the second when it came in my way, and gaze upon that which was enacted on the first, either laughingly or applausively. So, by degrees, the old-time fancies came back, and I began to believe there might be some delight in civilization after all. I saw a few friends, and, as I was not without money, made many new. Some of these have been really friends, and some of them—well! it would be useless to sum up their characters, as they were not the red devils I had latterly been brought in contact with. Possibly, none of them would have felt any pleasure in making my body serve as a living chandelier, by way of a prelude to lighting a bonfire with my person as the central faggot. Yet, very certainly, they would have cleaned me out of all I had about me, without the slightest compunction, not even allowing me to retain the price of one meal.

Amongst my old friends, I met Captain Crim, then a wealthy horse-dealer, dwelling on the Mission, and one whose word would have been good for thousands.

After our first interview, we dined together; and when I had given him a rough sketch of my adventurous life after he had left me at Susanville, we had a long talk over the events attending my first appearance on the Plains under my engagement with him. Many of the incidents which had occurred during it had almost been forgotten by me until he recalled them, and three or four of them were solemnized by a hearty roar of laughter upon my part, in which my old Captain joined with a will.

However, all pleasures must end. It was thus with my visit to the capital of the West.

After the first week of my stay in San Francisco, there is no doubt but that I began to enjoy the novelty of complete civilization thoroughly. Neither can there be any doubt but that complete civilization as thoroughly enjoyed me. In truth, in some three months it literally cleaned me out. An offer was made me of a brief engagement on the stage. But my first week's repugnance, when my pockets were not empty, had with their emptiness deepened into a strong disgust. Shaking off the dust from the soles, not of my feet, but my boots, in the spring, I again turned my face towards Honey Lake.

It need scarcely be affirmed that my little wife was glad enough to see me again. Without imputing to her any lack of affection, it may, however, be assumed that the Rangers were almost as pleased as she was, at my reappearance in Susanville. Brighton Bill, as I afterwards heard, said:

"Now, Hi'm blowed hif we shan't 'ave ha little fun. Mose his has good ha Cap for ha lark, has ha Hingun skrimmage."

Whether so or not, the boys rallied round me at once, and, greatly to my wife's disgust, commenced a series of plannings and plottings for the occupation of the ensuing summer and winter.

This year was commemorated by a very heavy emigration to Idaho by the way of Susanville, Surprise Valley, and Penabla Mountain. General Wright, who was on his way to the vicinity of the latter, for the purpose of prospecting with a party of some twelve men, had been specially recommended to me, and tarried with me for some four or five weeks.

After this, he had started in the direction of Penabla. For a considerable length of time no news came back to us, in any way, of his party. Naturally, this, at first, caused small uneasiness on our parts. Neither the Pony Express nor the Telegraph have yet penetrated every part of the great but sparsely settled West. In consequence of this, the lack of constant intelligence scarcely argued that the receipt of news must unmistakably be unpleasant, if not disastrous.

However, I chanced to be out with a party of the Rangers, on our way to the Humboldt River. We were near Black Rock, when we happened to meet an old Pah-ute Indian with several squaws, possibly or not, his own property. There was an appearance of a sort of Mormon respectability about the wrinkled red-skin, which at the moment impressed me, to a certain extent, favorably. Feeling this, I stepped up to him for the purpose of speaking. Judge what my astonisment was, when, drawing near him, to notice that he was smoking a pipe which I positively remembered as having been in the possession of the General.

There could not be the slightest mistake in this fact.

It was much too costly a pipe to have come into the possession of any Indian, save as a present, or by the more usual means in which the red-skin may acquire such property. My readers will very readily understand what such means are. Wright had himself told me how highly he valued this pipe. It had been presented to him by a dear friend, who was at this time dead. There must necessarily have been but small probability that it should have been a voluntary gift to the old Pah-ute.

Taking it at once from him, I demanded "where" he "got it."

"Me heap find em," was his leisurely reply. "Injin no steal 'em."

By this time, Bill Dow and several of the other Rangers had joined us. Dow also had happened to notice the pipe in the General's possession. With an angry imprecation, he exclaimed:

"Yer lie, yer red devil!" Then turning to me, he said: "Mose! as sure as God's in Heaven, that 'ere cuss has had a hand in killing Wright, for sartin. I reckon we'd jist better go over to Pabla, and look arter his party. Not, Cap! as I wants to dictate to yer. Only knowing as how the Gineral was a real friend of your'n, I thought, perhaps—"

"Thought!" I cried out, "Dow, when you know you are right."

"I'm dead sartin of it," he muttered between his teeth.

The aged Pah-ute had, while this was passing, been regarding me with that stoical indifference of feature which is so characteristic of the red man. Looking fixedly at him, I said:

"If you were not an old fellow, I would at once kill you. But if anything has gone wrong with the General or his party, see that you never again allow yourself to come within sight of me."

Immediately after this, we started for Summit Lake, and passing it, went down the cañon as far as the Puabla. On the following day about noon, we came to a cabin which had very evidently been occupied by Wright and his companions. It was now empty. . The small cañon in which this rough cabin stood was filled with cottonwood trees and a dense growth of small underbrush. As we were examining the place, I came upon the first fragmentary testimony of the dark tragedy which had branded this spot with an ineffaceable stain. This was the leg of a man, which had been hewn off just below the knee. While I was yet looking at it, Arnold called out in a tremulously hollow voice, which at once indicated from how intensely nervous an agitation he must be suffering:

"Come here, Mose."

He was but a short distance in advance of me; and when I arrived where he was standing, let me own that I frankly regretted not having cut the throat of the wrinkled old ruffian whose possession of the General's pipe had placed me on the track of this most dastardly and savage murder—aye! and the throats of all the squaws who were with him, too. Had I not, in my own person, had a sufficient experience of the gentleness of these she-devils? Could I doubt that it had been also displayed in the atrocious massacre of General Wright and the unfortunate men who had accompanied him?

I shall, of course, be asked for the full particulars of this ferocious butchery. Let me be as brief as I can in penning the details, which almost sicken me while I recall them.

We found the General actually spitted, a pointed stake having been forced lengthwise from behind through his body, and protruding beneath his chin. This stake had then been placed upon two crotched limbs of trees, above a fire, of which nothing but the dead embers now remained. As far as we could make out, there were no other marks of violence on the charred shape of the victim. He must have been killed by the terrible torture of thrusting this stake through his entrails. The remainder of his party had been literally cut into pieces. Arms, hands, heads, feet, legs, thighs, and bodies had been hewn apart, and were scattered around in the brush. Nor was there more than one of the victims who might have been slain before they were subjected to this inch by inch torture. Only a single wound by a bullet could be found by us, on any of these mutilated fragments of what had once been life.

And these brutal devils are the race that the Government of the United States demand should be dealt gently with by its children. I should refrain from denouncing them, perhaps, when the barbarities I had twice experienced at their hands are remembered by me. But in such a case as the present one, where my memory has no individual suffering to give it edge and bitterness, I may surely be permitted to express my opinions. This, the more specially, when I know that these opinions are shared in by every settler who has had some two or three years' practical dealing with the falsehood, rascality, treachery, blood-thirstiness, and demon-like barbarity, which, almost invariably, in every instance, characterize the Western Indian.

What, let me fearlessly ask, could in any way have been the natural result of the hesitation of the Government at Washington, to operate efficiently for the protection of its own children?

These men had, undoubtedly, the right to claim such a protection. Any other country to which they might have belonged, would have given it to them. It has, however, been consistently refused, or accorded them in a way which renders it worse than useless. They have, consequently, been compelled to rely upon themselves for protection, it being carried out after their own fashion. Necessarily, this fashion has varied. But, in no case, could it take a shape other than of the struggle ever-existent between the conflicting parties, when law has become paralyzed, or neglects to put in a satisfactory appearance. For many years, legal restraint had been overridden in San Francisco. At length, the condition of society resulting from this became unbearable. It was then that the citizens of the capital of the young and vigorous West took the matter into their own hands, independently of the State authorities. A vigilance committee sprung from their actual necessity, and, in a short space of time, daily crime was reduced to the ordinary ratio it bears in civilization. Even in the great Eastern metropolis, during the past two or three years, a similar necessity has been proclaimed, and a like exertion of the popular will has been predicted by some of the leading New York journals. There, however, law seems recently to have awakened from its long slumber, and, if consistently active and severe, will repress the lawlessness of passion or criminality.

But where there is no law, save on sparsely rare occasions, as is sufficiently evidenced on the mountains, and in the valleys and plains bordering on California, the action of vigilance committees, or some restraint as sharp and certain, is a paramount necessity.

How can it be wondered at, while crime of the nature of the last-mentioned, and others which I have recounted, are of well-nigh yearly occurrence, that it should have exerted, on the part of those exposed to its visitation—without the interference of national protection except at rare intervals—the determination to repress it, bloodily and mercilessly, as the instances in which it develops its own atrocity and pitilessness, too evidently require?

However, let me avoid the appearance of defending what I believe to be the righteous exertion of a spirit of self-protection, and leave it to the unbiassed judgment of my readers.

Burying the fragments of the bodies of the poor victims, or as many of them as we could find after a long and sorrowful search, in as decent a manner as we could, we resumed our way to the Humboldt. Here we located some six miles above Lancaster, on this river, and met with no very great success in our search for the precious metals. While here, an Indian from above Gravelly Ford, known by us as Shoshonee John, came in to our party. He could talk very fair English, and had been driven from his tribe in consequence of his openly professed friendly feeling to the whites. After a brief discussion among the boys, he was permitted to remain with us, until we started on our return. This was some time in August, in 1865.

We had reached the back of Granite Creek Station, which was then kept by Allen Simmons, from Oroville, and a man of the name of Bill Curry, when we fell in with some eight or ten Mahalas, with their papooses or children.

One of the Mahalas was a white woman. She had been taken by the Bannocks when she was no more than twelve years of age, in 1851. All her relatives and companions had been killed by them. Only herself had been spared. She was now married to a redskin, by whom, she told us, she had five children. On our asking her to leave her captors, with the tears standing in her eyes, she refused to do so. She said that she knew of no friends who would receive her. What, she did not attempt to disguise that she considered as the disgrace of her present life, would, as she felt, preclude her from all white friendship. In consequence of this, she avowed herself determined to remain. On being further questioned, she told us that we were the first white men she had seen since the period of her capture. I then asked her, if she had heard of the horrible massacre of General Wright and his party. Bursting into tears, she affirmed that it had been " the work of Smokecreek Sam, and the wretches who were with him."

Her grief and disgust at this were so marked and unmistakable, that I had no hesitation in asking her to tell us how and where we might find this scoundrel and his gang of ruffians. Without the slightest hesitation, she did so. Indeed, from the sudden flash in her eyes, and the rush of color to her tanned, yet still smooth cheeks, I felt convinced she experienced a bitter delight in believing that we might punish him. It is generally impossible for the necessity of life, or even for love, to blot out the ties of blood. She might be compulsorily a Mahala, yet was still, at heart, a white woman.

Again I endeavored to induce her to quit her present mode of life, but, unhesitatingly, although sadly, she refused to abandon the red-skin with whom her existence had been for so many years' linked, and his and her children.

At Granite Station, Al. Simmons gave us additional information respecting Smoke-creek Sam. He had a few days before surprised a party of Chinamen, between the Peuabla mountain and Owyhee River. Some sixty, in all of them, had been murdered by the gang. This had been effected, in a similar way to the cruel mode of death by which General Wright had perished.

Pushing on, therefore, to the military station at Smoke Creek, we detailed the circumstances of these bloody outrages to Captain Smith, who was then in command of it.

His horror at hearing of the last, and being made acquainted with the details of the first, by those who had seen the remains of the murdered party, was as thorough, almost, as ours had been. An arrangement with him was, in consequence, speedily concluded, by which we were to proceed to Susanville, and, after giving our horses and ourselves a few days' rest, return to the station. Thence we were to start, in company with himself and men, to inflict, if possible, a well-deserved and retributory punishment on Smoke-creek Sam and his gang.

On arriving at the station, we found a party of three or four men from the Humboldt, who had preceded us by a few hours.

They had brought the intelligence that a party of Indians had visited Granite Creek on the day before. The station, as they informed us, had been burned to the ground. Al. Simmons, Bill Curry, and another man, had been killed. When A. R. Le Roy, who had joined the Rangers previous to our leaving the Humboldt River, heard this, he was fearfully excited. Al. Simmons had been one of his dearest friends, and the news of this additional murder increased not only his rage, but that of all of us.

Captain Smith was by no means dilatory. His men were soon in their saddles, after we had rejoined him, and we pushed on rapidly to Granite Creek.

About one hundred yards west of the station, we found the body of Simmons, lying on his face upon the ground. A small bullet-hole was just outside of his heart. He must have been slain instantly. Myself and the other boys felt his death as keenly as we had done anything, for some time. Scarcely eight days since, we had been sitting with him, and talking of the butchery of the Chinese; and now we saw that his life had been sacrificed by the red devils as relentlessly, although in a less cowardly manner. As for Le Roy, when he saw the body, he flung himself on the ground beside it, and throwing his arms around the lifeless form of his friend, burst into a savage flood of tears. Within the burned-up timber of the station lay poor Curry, who had been slain there. The third man had evidently attempted to escape by flight. But the Indians had been too quick for him. Judging by their tracks, which were still clearly visible, he had been pursued, overtaken, and brought back. Less fortunate than the others, his death had not been so speedy. He had been stretched upon the earth with his face downwards. His hands and feet had been fastened by thongs to stakes driven into it. Brush and branches, hewn from the trees, had been then heaped upon his body and set fire to.

It would be unnecessary to say, that had anything been wanting to quicken our desire for retaliation, this must have done so. After attending to a hurried burial, we took the trail, which led us evidently in the direction the white Mahala had indicated to me, when I had asked her to tell me where Smoke-creek Sam and his gang were generally to be found.

Two days after, we camped for the night in a small valley in the mountains above Black Rock.

This valley was some six miles, or more, distant from an almost level piece of ground, to which the name of Soldier Meadows had been given.

After attending to the demands of our stomachs, for we had been on our own legs or those of our horses since daybreak, I went out with some other of the Rangers, as scouts, to discover if we were yet near the red-skins. Possibly an hour and a half may have elapsed, when some camp-fires were seen by me in the direction of the upper part of Queen's River. Shoshonee John had accompanied me, and detected them as quickly as I had done.

"Pah-ute Ingin!" he at once said.

"Or Smoke-creek Sam!" I could not help replying.

"All, heap same. Pah-ute as bad, only Smokycreek Sam some worse."

Without pausing to discuss his exceeding Irish summary of the merits of the original tribe, and those who had absconded or been expelled from it, we immediately returned to our camp, being joined upon our way by Butch' Hasbrouck, who had also detected the same campfires.

"How far off, Butch', did you believe the red-skins were?"

"Ten miles will bring yer to 'em."

"He right!" sententiously observed the Indian who had accompanied me.

My estimate of the distance agreed with theirs, and upon our reaching the camp, the Rangers immediately took to their saddles, and Captain Smith ordered his men to mount. While they were doing this the redskin addressed me, saying:

"Give Shoshonee John a gun, to help shoot heap Pah-utes."

"How do I know you will?"

The question was prompted by the knowledge I had acquired of the Indian character. It seemed to me that if the petitioner had owned a gun at the time about which he first joined us, he might, not improbably, have kept out of our neighborhood. He, however, answered me promptly enough.

"Pah-ute Ingin heap shoot Shoshonee John when catch him. Shoshonee John shoot him, too."

It might be so. But Harry Arnold and Ben Painter took the same view of the case as I did, and the matter was compromised by Captain Smith ordering him to be given a cavalry sabre. At the same time, Brighton Bill, who had been listening, growled out:

" 'E's ha convarted red devil. IIi'm blamed hif II'i wouldn't 'a given 'im a rifle."

When within a mile or something more of the camp, a halt was ordered, while some of us made a reconnoissance. Creeping up to their position, we found the band must count heavily. It had encamped on the very edge of the desert, which was here some forty miles across, without a single bush or shrub growing upon it. It formed almost a dead level, and in the dry season was so hard that a horse would scarcely leave the slightest track by which scout or red-skin could have trailed it.

CHAPTER XIX.

A LIVELY COMMENCEMENT—THE FIGHT IN THE DESERT—EXTERMINATION OF A BAND OF CUT-THROATS—THE CAVALRY SABRE—A CONTRAST—PERMITTED TO RETIRE AND RECEIVING PROMOTION—A LITTLE LOVE—CHANCE AND TROUBLE—WHAT CAME OF IT—"SMOKING OUT A VARMINT"—A FEW PRISONERS—THE INDIAN AGENT—NEW FRUIT ON A TREE—ALONE ON A TRAIL—THE END.

AFTER a brief council, in which Captain Smith, Harry Arnold, and myself were the principal ones who took a part, it was determined to surround them on the side where we then were, and immediately day had broken, to drive them to the desert. By doing this, we calculated scarcely one of them would have a chance of escaping.

"At last, Mose!" said Le Roy, who happened to be near me, "we have the blood-thirsty devils! and may God not spare me, if I fail to kill, while a single one of them is left alive."

He scarcely seemed to be aware of the meaning of his muttered words. But I knew of what he was thinking. It was of the death of Al. Simmons.

In some forty minutes the necessary orders had been given, and we had advanced nearly within gun-shot of them. We had moved into our position with the most complete silence. What had startled the Indians, I was and still am unable to imagine. They had, however, discovered our approach, and yelling out their war-whoop, dashed towards us, on our centre. It was just light enough for them to make out our strength. When they found this, they recoiled, and, almost at the same instant, made a charge upon our left. For some few minutes the boys and soldiers on that side of our position had lively work, and then, finding out that there also we were too strong for them, the red-skins started out on the desert.

We pursued them leisurely for some six miles. Then putting the spur to our horses, we galloped up and surrounded them.

It was now daylight. We could see the work before us.

Justice must be done even to such a rascally set of murdering thieves as Smoke-creek Sam's gang. When caught, they did fight, as I honestly believe no Pah-utes have ever before done. However, the blue-coated servants of Uncle Sam and the Buckskin Rangers fought better. The soldiers rode amongst the red-skins, hewing them down with their sabres, while our boys were equally busy with revolver and knife.

This had scarcely been going on for as many minutes as we had covered miles of the desert, when I marked one Indian. From descriptions of Smoke-creek Sam, which we had almost all of us heard, I determined that this must be the scoundrel, and rode up to him. I was lying on the side of my horse when he saw me. Lifting his revolver, he fired three or four shots at me as rapidly as he could.

The last of these crashed through the skull of the noble brute, that had borne me so well and gallantly for so many years. I felt, even at the moment in which he fell—in spite of the enemy who were in the front and on all sides of me—a cruel pang.

It so happened that when I fell, Arnold was near me

and had seen the shot take effect on the animal I was mounted on. He knew how greatly I valued the gift of Jack Bird, not simply on acount of the giver, but on its own account. I heard his voice, as the report of his own pistol rang on the ear, almost immediately following that of the red-skin's. Giving utterance to a fierce cry, he yelled out:

"You have killed the Tipton Slasher. Take that, you red devil!"

Harry's ball had broken the right arm of Smoke-creek Sam, and he had gone to grass as it struck him, or, at all events, I thought so. The red ruffian had certainly fallen, and, extricating myself from the panting body of my dying horse, I leapt towards him for the purpose of raising his hair. While I was in the act of doing this, I saw that he was not yet dead. With a desperate clutch of his left hand, he was trying to grasp the revolver which had fallen from his maimed limb upon the ground. It was lying a trifle beyond his reach, and before I had time even to think of putting him out of his misery, I saw the gleam of a cavalry sabre flashing through the air.

The blade fell.

In another instant, the savagely brutal head of Smoke-creek Sam was hanging from his shorn neck, attached to it merely by a small portion of bleeding flesh. At the same moment when this was effected, a voice shrieked out:

"Buckeeskin Mose, he now see whether Shoshonee John fight. Think him kill heap."

There was clearly no more reason for doubting the sincerity of our Indian ally.

"Smoke-creek Sam?"

This demand was made by me with an inquiring gesture, as, in doing so, I extended to him the scalp I had just lifted. Looking first at it, and then at the head he had so nearly severed from the body it belonged to, as if to make sure of their former connection, he replied:

"Heap sure."

The answering affirmative was uttered with a sententious gravity, exemplarily characteristic of his red ascestry, as Cooper has painted similar races long since wiped out by our rushing civilization. Striding from us, he then looked around the battle-field for more of his brethren, upon whom he could display the reality of his detestation of them, as well as his capacity as a headsman.

However, by this time the strife was well-nigh over. Not one of Smoke-creek Sam's gang could be seen standing upon his feet. The hard soil of the desert, for more than quarter of a mile square, was strown with their dead bodies. Eighty-one of the merciless scoundrels had paid with an honorable end for their bloodily disgusting crimes. Not a single red-skin had escaped from the bullet or the sabre. The band of torturing and villanous cut-throats and murderers had been totally exterminated.

In this instance also, I can justly say, as I have done in Colonel Connor's battle on Bear River, that Captain Smith, although an officer in the regular service, did his work well and thoroughly.

The Pah-utes, however, had not been reduced to tranquillity. As I have earlier explained, this gang was merely a section of that tribe whose atrocities and lawlessness had compelled their expulsion from it. Not, indeed, their atrocity and lawlessness against us, the

12*

white settlers, but that which they displayed at the expense of their red brethren.

Scarcely had I returned and been, for a short time, in the society of my little wife, settled down in Susanville, when an incident occurred which fully demonstrated this fact.

At this time, a body of Uncle Sam's blue-coats were stationed in the vicinity of Summit Lake. The cavalry was under the command of Captain Hall, and the infantry under that of Captain Meyers. It happened that two of our most prominent citizens were crossing the mountains, some four miles nearer than this post, when they were attacked by a party of red-skins. The leg of one of them, named Kesler, was broken by a rifle-ball at the first volley aimed at them by the attacking Indians. The other of the men was possessed of cool courage and indomitable pluck. This was Frank Drake. No sooner did he see his companion fall, than he asked briefly:

"Are you wounded?"

"The red cusses have broken my leg, Drake!"

"Yer must be off, then."

"How on airth can I?"

"We'll soon see," cried Frank cheerily.

Cutting one of the horses loose from their team, he helped Kesler on to it, in spite of the bullets which were rattling on the other side of the wagon. Then, bidding him ride to the Lake to ask for assistance from the soldiers, he proposed to fight it out alone with the Indians. Kesler remonstrated vainly with him. Giving to the horse he had cut loose a heavy lash with the whip he had previously been using, he said:

"Go, yer darned fool, unless yer wish both on us to be done for, by the red skunks."

The animal started with Kesler, followed by a pelting shower of bullets. None of them, however, struck either him or the horse. This unusual hint, in all probability, accelerated the speed of the latter, for he seems to have made good time. In about twenty minutes, Kessler arrived at the place where the blue-coats were stationed, and on seeing Captain Hall, told him the situation in which he had left Frank Drake, and begged him to send his friend "help at once." This officer replied in the usual official slang of the Plains:

"I've lost no Indians, and I'll be hung, if I'm going to trot out my men for nothing."

"Nothing! Hain't I told yer Frank Drake is fighting the red devils, by himself?"

"By this time," was Hall's reply, "the man is killed. We shan't find him."

In spite of this refusal, in which Uncle Sam's servant persisted, some few of his men, accompanied by several settlers who chanced to be present, at once mounted their horses and galloped off, leaving Kesler behind, to have his leg attended to by the army surgeon, if the post rejoiced in such an appendage. This is by no means invariably the case. The party galloping to save the plucky Frank Drake, made even better speed than his companion had done.

No sooner were their rapidly advancing hoofs heard, than the cowardly Indians fled.

Upon arriving at the point where the team had been left standing, they, at first, saw no living creature save one of the remaining horses. Frank Drake was found by them stretched under the wagon. When the red-skins ran, he knew relief was at hand, and had fainted away from loss of blood. Wounded in almost every part of his body as he was, by great luck, not one of the holes made by the Pah-utes was dangerous. Two of them were lying dead on the farther side of the road; and when he revived, he told those who had rescued him he thought he had seen a third of them carried away as they were approaching.

The preceding incident of frontier life is mentioned by me for the purpose of striking a just balance with regard to the protection afforded the settlements by the Government. This will be the better appreciated by the reader, when he hears I have been told that Captain Smith was "permitted to retire," while Captain Hall has since received the reward due to his services, by promotion.

Let me, before closing this volume, relate another incident which displays, in an even more striking light, the love for Uncle Sam's relatives which is so very generally exhibited by his servants.

Some time in 1865 or 1866, a family had moved into Honey Lake Valley consisting of an old man and his wife, with a daughter, whose charming face and winning manners might have entitled her to a place in far better society than Susanville could by any possibility afford her. The name of the family was Pierson. Their child was called Hattie. They had settled on a ranche just below Laithrop's place and near the Hot Springs. Butch' Hasbrouck had, shortly after the family arrived, become acquainted with them, and greatly to the pleasure of the parents, had made arrangements to reside under their roof.

Of course, such fair readers as I may not have terrified into closing this volume, by the too bloody tales I have written out in these pages, will readily enough divine the reason which had led him so quickly into an intimacy with the parents and their daughter.

Hasbrouck loved Hattie Pierson.

He had, I believe, told me, only, of his happiness when he became engaged to her. Certainly, it was not generally known. She was still so young, that her father had insisted upon the marriage being deferred until the following year.

In the meantime, Hattie's beauty had attracted other admirers.

These she had managed to make understand that she did not love them, without inflicting upon them, or her own kindly and gentle nature, the pain of a refusal. One of them was, however, more obstinately pertinacious. This was a man of the name of Cockrell, who, in spite of every hint she had given him, persisted in his attentions, and at last made her an offer of marriage. Being thus cornered, as it were, the girl was compelled to refuse him. In the hope of softening her refusal by giving him a positive reason for it, she blushingly owned that she was engaged to Butch' Hasbrouck. She had learnt to give him the same appellation which all his friends had so long done.

What was her horror when Cockrell burst into a furious fit of passion, not only reproaching her in the vilest manner, but swearing not only to kill him but the girl also.

When this occurred, Butch' had been absent with the Rangers. This was only for a short time, and on his return, Hattie told him how Cockrell had terrified her. Her lover comforted her by laughing away her fears.

However, on the next day, he made his appearance where I was living, and asked me to go with him in search of this man.

"What for, Butch'?" I asked.

"Nare yer mind, Mose! When I find the darned cuss, yer'll know, soon enough."

Of course, I went with him. But our search was a fruitless one. Cockrell had disappeared from Susanville the day before. No sooner had he heard that the Rangers had returned than he had quitted the place. When Hasbrouck found that this was positively so, he frankly told me the reason which induced him to search for the fellow.

"But if you had found him, Butch', what was it you meant to do?"

"What war it I meant to do? In course, shoot the darned blackguard."

Up to this moment, he had been as cool as a cucumber, or, rather, as the winter snow on Bear River during my campaign in that locality. Your quiet men are always dangerous, and so I told him. At the same time, I consoled him with the reflection that Cockrell's conduct had proved this fact. After abusing little Hattie Pierson like a dastardly cur, he had cleared out, immediately after the return of her plighted lover.

"P'raps yer're right, Mose!"

"I know I am, my boy! A white liver always tells. So has his."

"The varmint has run tu the nearest hole he could find," he said with a smile.

"If we catch him, we'll smoke him out."

We both laughed, and we were both wrong to laugh. In the following year, we again went upon the Humboldt, and shortly after we had done so, old Mr. Pierson decided to move further south, to Winamucca Valley, near Red Rock. When the family were passing up the east side of Honey Lake, they were attacked by Indians and all of them were murdered. When found, the body of the old man was literally riddled with bullets. Mrs. Pierson and Hattie were lying in each other's arms, clasped tightly, as if in the effort to shield each other from death. They had been slain in the same manner.

Intelligence of this was brought to us. And I can never forget the effect it had upon Butch' Hasbrouck when he heard it.

His face became lividly white, in spite of the tanning by exposure it had so long had. Without a word, he turned, lifted his rifle and his shot-pouch, took a small bag which he filled with parched corn, and was leaving us. Throwing my arm around his neck, I said:

"Where are you going?"

"After them as killed my Hattie."

"Do you think I shall not go with you?" I asked.

"Hand Il'i too?" exclaimed Brighton Bill.

Arnold and Painter were already preparing to accompany him, and, in less than an hour, we were all upon the homeward road.

Our search was, for some two weeks, completely in vain. Although, near the scene of the murder, keen eyes could make out the trail, it was lost at a short distance from it, owing to the rocky nature of the soil. However, where we had first seen it, Butch' affirmed that he had discovered the track of a white man. Arnold and myself thought as he did. If so, this man was Cockrell. The belief in this fact made Hasbrouck untiring in his attempt to recover the trail.

In spite of every effort on his part and ours, we were unable to do so. It was a providential chance which enabled us, at last, to fasten upon a portion of the guilty parties. These were, unfortunately, all red-skins.

One morning, while on Willow Creek, we fell in with five Pah-utes. It was a surprise party both for them and us, and a luckless surprise for the red-skins. There was no chance for their showing fight. We were nearly five times their own number. Neither could they fly; we had surrounded them. Butch' had at once recognized upon them portions of old Pierson's clothing and some of Hattie's trinkets. We could not shoot them down in cold blood, and after a brief council, decided upon disarming and taking them with us as prisoners to Susanville. Had Cockrell been with them, I honestly believe he would never have left the spot alive. Hasbrouck would certainly have slain him where he stood. Nevertheless, he made no opposition to our present purpose. In his horror and wrath at the crime of the white scoundrel, he seemed to pass over that of the red devils who had aided him in accomplishing it, as scarcely worthy of notice.

Accordingly, they were taken to Susanville and placed in a species of lock-up which there did duty as a jail.

As we quitted Willow Creek, it may perhaps be mentioned that one of the red ruffians appealed to us to let him go, on the score that he had done nothing but "shoot him gun into old white man." This plea of innocence was necessarily unattended to.

We had intended to give them a fair trial, and it was to come off very quickly. It is only in large cities that justice is slow and dilatory. But on the morning immediately preceding the day which had been fixed for it, I mean the second morning of their imprisonment, Harry Arnold, in company with Butch' Hasbrouck, met me. It was in front of J. I. Steward's hotel. The former said:

"Cap! we were coming to see you."

"What is up now?"

He had given me the rank I had held when out with the Rangers. This he seldom did, even then, unless we were in active and trying pursuit of the red-skins. What did it mean?

"Wall, Mose, du yer want the infarnal red cusses who helped murder my Hattie to git clean off?" demanded Butch'.

"Certainly not!"

"Shut up, Butch'," exclaimed Harry, "until we are somewhere, where none can hear a word you are saying."

"Ye're jist right. I will."

When Arnold spoke last, I noticed that his strong fingers had grasped the arm of his companion, tightly. Moreover, I was enabled to remark that the face of the latter had more of its old vitality. This was, however, at present, by no means of an alluringly agreeable character. His eyes seemed to have the very devil in them. When he replied to Harry, he strode rapidly up the street. Arnold and myself followed him, until we had passed the last house or log shanty in it, and had reached a clear and open spot. Here I came to a dead halt.

"And now, man, what is it you have to tell me?"

"Du yer know the skunk the folks in Washington sent to Pyramid Lake, last fall, as *Injun agint?"

---

* Unfortunately, I am unable to recall the name of this individual, and therefore cannot pillory it.

"Yes!"

"What d'yer think he's a' goin' tu du with the cuss'd red devils we cotched up thar," as he said this, he gave a jerk with his thumb in the direction leading to it, "at Willer Crik?"

"What can he do with them?"

"He's a' goin' to rin 'em off to-morrer, on to the Resarvation. So we can't du nothing with them," Hasbrouck replied savagely.

"You must be dreaming, Butch'," I exclaimed angrily. "The thieving scoundrel doesn't dare do it."

"Doesn't he?" asked Arnold, with a bitter smile. "Why! he isn't even one of Uncle Sam's bluecoats!"

Arnold then explained to me how the other Ranger had learned that this plan had actually been decided upon, and gave me the names of some of our more timidly loyal fellow-citizens, who had been induced by the agent to guarantee him their support. What was there for us to do? This fellow actually represented our respected Uncle! He had probably called for the assistance of the regulars stationed in the vicinity of Susanville. Little doubt, perhaps, existed in our minds that our boys could have whipped them with the help of their friends, who, I firmly believe, would have turned out in mass, at such a call as we might have made. But this would have been insurrection, or treason, or something of the sort. I could see nothing left for us to do, but to grin and bear it. That was a natural necessity.

But somehow or other, on that night the matter was removed from our hands, as well as that of the Indian agent aforesaid. While we were all sleeping the sound slumber of law-abiding citizens of the United States, a party of masked men overpowered the jailer, and broke into the prison.

On the next morning, a fine tree which stood at the side of Albert Smith's dwelling-house bore a new kind of fruit. The red-skins who had murdered Hattie Pierson and her parents were dangling from its branches. They had paid for their crime with its legitimate penalty.

It was a sound and vigorous specimen of frontier justice.

Suspicion pointed its finger at many of my fellow-citizens, possibly, myself included. The Indian agent was furious. But the perpetrators of this act of justice, outside of law, kept their own counsel. Up to the present, as I have reason to know, suspicion has failed to obtain positive proof of the hands that hung the five Pah-ute assassins.

This volume is now drawing to a close, as in 1869 I quitted that portion of the country in which I had so long been residing. Nevertheless, in the preceding year, one more bloody act occurred which it may be necessary to record. Hiram Partridge and Vesper Coburn were at this period keeping the station at Deep Hole Springs, to which my pilgrimage in the winter of 1861 with lame Tom Bear may be remembered by any one who has not shrunken from my company up to the present time. Hiram was a cousin of John Partridge, and had once been a partner with me in working my claim at the mines on the Humboldt. Vesper Coburn was an old schoolfellow and playmate of mine, when we were no more than children. Consequently, I no sooner heard of their murder than I determined, were it within my power, to avenge it.

Previous to this, the organization of the Buckskin Rangers had been broken up.

Susanville had somewhat declined from its old prosperity. If the settlement round Honey Lake had been growing at all, it was certainly not doing so, at its right end. Montana had sprung into sudden prominence, Idaho was greatly increasing in wealth and the number of its inhabitants, while other places in the surrounding section of the country, to the south and west, were rapidly outstripping us. Many of my old comrades had gone to the two places I have more distinctly named, while some of them had struck on beyond, as far as Lower California.

When this outrage occurred, I chanced to be at Reno, a small town on the line of the Central Pacific Railroad, which was then completed as far as Salt Lake City. It is at Reno the junction is now formed with the line for Virginia City, Nevada.

Some months had passed subsequent to the death of Partridge and Coburn, when I encountered three redskins in the vicinity of this place, and recognized the horse on which one of them was mounted as Hiram's property. Beside this, they all of them wore articles of clothing which were decidedly not made by the Indians. Had anything else been wanting to convince me of their being the criminals, this was supplied by my personal knowledge of the faces of two of them. These had been in the actual employment of the murdered men.

They started on their return to the mountains, and I followed them.

My pursuit only counted one white, all told—myself. Their number was triple mine. The odds were sufficient to justify the weaker party in employing stratagem. Suffice it that I did so, and counted three scalps against the deaths of my old playmate and recent partner.

If any doubt had been entertained by me of the justice of this action, it would have been speedily dispelled by the additional proof shortly after afforded me. It was only a few days after my return to the Humboldt, that a red-skin, known by me as Pah-ute Jim, accused me of killing his brother, one of the two Indians who had been employed by my murdered friends.

"Yes!" I unhesitatingly answered. "I did kill him, because he helped to kill Partridge and Coburn."

"Umph!" he ejaculated. "Natches heap tell 'um kill. No kill, Natches heap kill Injin."

Natches, I ought possibly to mention, was, at this time, the chief of the Pah-utes.

With this incident, I may fairly conclude. My Indian hunting, trapping, and fighting ended with it. Since this I have been engaged in mining and other pursuits, having resided for some length of time in Salt Lake City among the Mormons. Should my first literary venture, my dear reader, prove tolerably successful, Heaven only can tell whether it may not be followed by another. If so, it is just within the range of possibility, I may turn from Indian fighting to Mormon polygamy. I can scarcely say which you may think the least interesting. But I can honestly vouch for it, the many-wife business will be the most amusing.

www.ingramcontent.com/pod-product-compliance
Lightning Source LLC
Chambersburg PA
CBHW022101230426
43672CB00008B/1247